FROM LITTLE AC

# FROM LITTLE
# ACORNS

*With love to*

*P...heng*

## An Autobiography by
## Graeme Whiting

*Graeme W.*

22

Proverb:

Great oaks from little acorns grow.

'My children flourished at The Acorn School. Acorn teaching helped them blossom into well-rounded, self-confident adults. I am deeply grateful to Graeme for his fearless dedication to finding the promise in each student.'

*(JM, Acorn parent)*

For more information about Graeme Whiting
or The Acorn School go to:

www.graemewhiting.com

www.theacornschool.com

ISBN 9781914424694
Published by YouCaxton Publications 2022

YouCaxton Publications
www.youcaxton.co.uk

Cover design by Jason Conway

Front Cover Photo:
David Whiting, aged 10 and Graeme Whiting, aged 7 (L to R) (Norfolk, 1951)

Back Cover Photos:
The Acorn School main building, Nailsworth (in background)
Graeme Whiting (2021)

For my wife, Sarah, and my children who have been educated by their parents and have demonstrated that this cutting-edge education works.

# The Road Not Taken

Two roads diverged in a yellow wood,
And sorry I could not travel both
And be one traveler, long I stood
And looked down one as far as I could
To where it bent in the undergrowth;

Then took the other, as just as fair,
And having perhaps the better claim,
Because it was grassy and wanted wear;
Though as for that the passing there
Had worn them really about the same,

And both that morning equally lay
In leaves no step had trodden black.
Oh, I kept the first for another day!
Yet knowing how way leads on to way,
I doubted if I should ever come back.

I shall be telling this with a sigh
Somewhere ages and ages hence:
Two roads diverged in a wood, and I—
I took the one less traveled by,
And that has made all the difference.

ROBERT FROST (1874–1963)

# CONTENTS

# FOREWORD

I am delighted to be writing this foreword to a book that Graeme Whiting has talked about writing for many years. It also allows me the opportunity to express some gratitude to a close friend who I first met on an open day visit to the Rudolf Steiner school where Graeme was my daughter Rachel's Year 8 teacher at the time. I was immediately welcomed into the classroom with a positive and open greeting from him which included a stirring appraisal of a recent drawing that Rachel had made. 'Now THAT is a horse!' he said.

The strength of his conviction in the field of education was immediately apparent to me and after volunteering to accompany Graeme and his class on a school ski trip to Austria, during which we had many deeply interesting talks together, we soon became good friends. We discovered a shared interest in fishing which also led to many more conversations together sitting in nature beside various rivers, ponds and lakes.

It is a rare thing in life to find a true and reliable friend who always maintains a positive attitude no matter what. Graeme and I met at a time in my life when career and family duties were taking their toll on my energy, and he came into my life as a much needed breath of fresh air.

I know that it was not easy for him to follow the craggy path of an educational pioneer and go through long periods of real hardship to manifest his vision of The Acorn School. In this endeavour there was no room for compromise as he was setting new standards in the field of education, and there will always be resistance to real change in any established field. I am proud to say that I was fortunate to have played a small part in helping to launch the school in those early days, but the magic and vision all came through Graeme's determination to make his own dream a living reality.

    This book is a true life adventure story which I suggest you savour as you might a simple glass of wine by the fireside while watching the slowly fading embers on a cosy winter's evening.

    Terry Oldfield (July 2021)

# PREFACE

After many decades as a teacher and father of five children, I looked across my sitting room one evening, and my gaze centred on my wonderful wife, Sarah.

After a few seconds I saw, as William Blake saw in his dedicated wife, Kate, the face of an angel who has stood by my side for almost fifty years in daily determination to give children a child-centred education far removed from the education systems offered today which generate an environment of needless competition, causing anxiety and the requirement to compete child against child.

Together, we have embraced the vision that is manifest in the school we created.

From soldier to public schoolteacher and into Steiner education, I have taken the road less travelled and my inspiration lies in that beautiful poem by Robert Frost, 'The Road Not Taken.'

My road has been less travelled, but as I write this book I realise that what has been created in The Acorn School is necessary for the entire human world.

# CHAPTER 1

# WINTERTON

I was born in Hereford on 3 August 1944, at the end of WWII, the eighth child of nine; six boys and three girls.

My father, William, was in both the British Army in the Welsh Guards, and later on, in early 1944, he was transferred to The Royal Air Force before being demobbed as injured. My mother, Winifred, was in neither and was a saint.

Both parents were in service after the first world war, my father as a butler and my mother, a head cook. They fell in love when they were children in the Church school in Much Dewchurch near Hereford, a little red stone school building next to the local churchyard in which my grandparents were laid to rest. In an extraordinary coincidence, I later accepted a teaching post in that same school building where my parents played as children.

I tend to be somewhat meticulous, for example in setting a table properly for meals, making sure my shoes are shiny, and preparing food with care. It seems to me that in this, I mirror the impeccable habits my father learned at 'butler school'. He served lords, ladies, kings and queens in some stunning places, a few of which I later visited on game shooting Saturdays. On those visits I was often filled with wonder at how my father had ended up living and working in the 'downstairs' world; but perhaps this was a tribute to his and my mother's copious skills.

For a few years my parents were butler and head cook at a large country house in Hope under Dinmore, near Hereford. The house had an impressive square courtyard and despite numerous alterations over the centuries, it retained its original form. In my eyes, my parents should have been lord and lady of that lovely mansion instead of undertaking servants' tasks; but I have been graced by what my mother and father learned in service. My parents enjoyed their work and were complimentary about the owners during their time there. Their many stories about all the comings and goings have made me feel proud of my humble origins, especially my parents' willingness to serve at a time when the world was in a bit of a mess.

At that time The Great Depression was looming, The Versailles Treaty was instrumental in quaking the very ground on which Germany stood, and there was immense hardship throughout the world, which my parents recounted whenever I questioned them about those difficult years. It would be a real treat to be able to sit by a fire with them now and hear more about the aristocratic families, the things that went on downstairs, and their decision to leave their life in service and begin a family in 1926.

My mother's maiden name was Edwards, and her mother, my grandmother, was a Prosser, a well-known Herefordshire name. I never met my grandparents, and to redress my not having known a grandfather I have frequently stood as a grown-up at the graves of my mother's brothers in the military cemetery of Étaples, at Le Touquet, contemplating their surnames carved on the stone crosses. I've been able to read a poem at their gravesides many times, as I visited the cemetery every other year with my students. I think of it as an honouring of my roots and have taken all my children there.

I had a rather underprivileged, and what might be considered to have been poverty-stricken, upbringing; nevertheless vast amounts of love and understanding were showered on me by my devoted parents. Despite the fact that we were very poor, I grew up with joyful and exciting memories of our home life. My parents were inwardly beautiful people, and I see them as much more illustrious now they're no longer with me than when I was growing up in their loving care. Isn't that always the way? We never fully appreciate our parents until they have gone, and I certainly never declared my love for them when they were clipping me round the ear!

In 1947, when I was three, my family moved to Winterton-on-Sea, a small fishing village on the east coast of Norfolk, eight miles from Great Yarmouth and situated between the villages of Horsey to the north and Hemsby to the south. We made the big move there from Hereford as my mother had asthma, and her doctor suggested that the sea air of Norfolk might alleviate her condition.

After the war my father was given the opportunity to either receive a pension of ten shillings a week, index linked for life, or a lump sum of £750. He elected to take the lump sum and bought a lovely dilapidated run-down and condemned old stone cottage by the sea at Winterton. He paid the princely sum of £500 for Stone Cottage, and my father's decision ensured that we had our own home. For the next three years, eleven of us lived in this two-bedroomed little house which seemed like a palace to us. Although my father knew it was due to eventually be demolished, it was our family home for this memorable time, and we loved it.

Stone Cottage was an old fisherman's dwelling, two hundred yards from the sea with a small garden, a primitive 'thunderbox' for a lavatory and a well in the garden for all our water needs. One of my fondest memories is of dropping the wooden metal hoop-banded bucket that my father handcrafted, into the deep well and then winding it up full of sparkling water. I wondered how such pure and clear water could come from such a dark hole. We also pumped water into our wooden buckets from a standpipe which stood about three hundred yards from our cottage and served the village in times of drought. That task became weekly whenever there was a water shortage, and it was a laborious job as we needed countless gallons of water for our large family.

The cottage was a simple oak-framed fifteenth century whitewashed building, with the shapes of the stones easily visible, and here and there some flint stones inlaid for strength. Inside, there was one downstairs room and a rickety staircase that took us up to the two bedrooms. As we ran up the stairs, they creaked and we could feel the cottage swaying slightly. The walls were papered with pink roses on green ferns, which gave the impression of being in a wood. The roof never leaked, despite the fact that it was thatched, and I remember my father paying a lot of attention to making sure that the reeds he cut from the local Breydon Water were straight and strong enough for him to slide them easily into the roof whilst withdrawing the few that needed replacing. My father was also a self-declared thatcher.

The bedrooms were tightly set out. Mum, dad, my three sisters and I occupied the smaller room with the children on the floorboards, whilst those still at home, which they all were until 1950, squeezed into the other bedroom. They sometimes slept on the floor when an unexpected guest arrived, as my mother often took in a stray or two from the street – mostly those who had lost their way after the war. We all slept top to tail. I can see the boys lying there now as I peeped inside early one morning to see Michael with his toes up David's nose; the smell was acrid and the shouts of 'Get out!' made me frightened to peer in any further.

Our primitive shaky beds were always neatly made up with thin blankets and no sheets. With up to four in a bed, it was extraordinarily cramped and itchy, though cosier when Corona bottles filled with hot water were added between the blankets for winter warmth. These hot water bottles quickly cooled, so we would cuddle them against our scrawny bodies as soon as we got into bed, always fighting over whose turn it was to hold onto the biggest surface area. If the bottles weren't held close through the night, it got quite cold as every degree of heat drained out of them. But if we kept cuddling them, they would still be warm when we woke up in the morning. None of us could understand that phenomenon of physics!

My father cadged some ancient wardrobes from the other villagers, as one did in those days, and restored them into fine pieces of furniture. The kitchen table was tiny by today's standards, with nine of us crammed around it on stools whilst mum and dad sat on chairs at either end. My mother prepared the bread and dripping and tea-sop, and space was at a premium. The stools, though wobbly, were repaired often and were very well made by my father. The back garden was small and yet it seemed big enough as the cottage was detached. My father told me that the building had been declared unfit for habitation twenty years before we moved in, but we weren't to tell anyone.

I loved my cottage home and was oblivious to the lung damage being inflicted by the smoke-filled rooms. I still remember the smell of cigarette smoke filling our house, for as was common in those days, my father was a heavy smoker. We owned a cast-iron Brighton stove in which my parents burned the wood gathered by us children from around our house and the local woods. All our saucepans adorned this lovely warm heater, which continually burned and never broke down, even though it was alight throughout the year. I can still recall the hot cosy smell of the open fire and stove, occasionally burning with coke, though more often smouldering with hardwood logs and anything we could find.

In one corner of our downstairs kitchen-come-living room, sat the 'copper', in which my mother boiled the washing, the 'blue-bags' (laundry whiteners) that went into it, the sturdy old mangle, and the shapely homemade wooden clothes pegs, hand carved by my father and made to last forever. The mangle was my mother's pride and joy, and I was fascinated by it. One day, in my curiosity to discover how the mechanism worked, mum found that along with the wet clothes, she was also mangling my small hand, and she had to rewind to release me! My mother did a pile of washing for our family every day, added to which, she took in other people's washing and ironing, using a flat iron heated on the stove.

I wish I could return to that beloved cottage now and relive the memories of my time there as a young child – but it was knocked down some years ago to create a public house car park. I would love to touch the walls of the kitchen and stand where the mangle once stood, poised ever ready to squeeze the water out of our well-worn, mostly hand-me-down clothes; and to touch the Brighton stove where my mother cooked. Those straitened times were to enable me to overcome many hardships later on when I was a married man; and the older I get, the ever more loudly those early days seem to ring in my ears.

One of my earliest childhood memories is of the 'Waller-men' who came every few weeks or so to empty the outside lavatory, sucking up our family's smelly excrement through a long, flexible pipe aimed down the hole in the garden which was our lavatory, and depositing the foul-smelling contents into a large lorry. We all looked on with our faces shrouded by dirty hands cupped over our mouths and noses. It was like a giant unstoppable anaconda, writhing to find its way down that narrow hole into the dark and stinking abyss and steered by two grimacing men. The stench sent most families to the sea to escape the putrid air that was a feature of 'lavvy day'. I never wanted to be a lavvy man when I grew up!


Another clear early image is of the shiny buttons and the white belt and gaiters adorning the uniform of my oldest brother, William, who had been called up for service in the Royal Navy towards the end of WWII.

William (Bill) was born in 1926, and was aged eighteen when I came into the world in 1944. The second child was my oldest sister, Joan (1930), fourteen years older than me. Next was John (1931), thirteen years above me. Then came Reg (1932), twelve years my senior and after Reg was Kim (1935), my second sister, aged nine when I was born. The two brothers just above me were Michael (Mick), (1939), five years older than me, and David (1941), three years older. Finally, in 1947, three years after my birth, came the third girl, the ninth and last child, my younger sister, Dawn.

The twenty-one year span between the births of the nine children was enormous, and my parents needed to be determined and resourceful to give us all a secure upbringing. With such a sizeable brood and many strong personalities in the family, it was a noisy household; although the numbers thinned out as the older ones left home and began to marry. Inevitably, there was a level of chastisement meted out at home which I know was considered normal back then. In those days there was a common belief that younger children should be seen and not heard, so the smaller ones could feel like fairly insignificant members of the pack. My sisters took an interest in me, still I often found myself hiding behind a facade and inventing tall stories in order to seek recognition from the older ones in the family who I looked up to.

My three sisters, Joan, Kim and Dawn, were loving and kind to me, and I had a particularly close connection with my younger sister, Dawn, who I called Dawnie. My youngest two brothers, Michael and David, both a few years older than me and serving as my nearest role models, enjoyed teasing me and convinced me that under my bed was a murderer holding a blood-stained dagger and in the wardrobe was a ghost. I was relieved to find out by the time I was a teenager that they'd only been pulling my leg.

The care and diligence of my parents and the closeness of the family meant that we treasured our home and spent a lot of time together chatting, singing, and playing cards and board games. There was much fun and laughter between us, and I learned a great deal from my siblings. From an early age I would also often leave the house by myself to go off and have adventures with friends; though of course it was always gratifying when my older brothers were friendly towards me as they caught sight of me lurking in the dunes.

As a close-knit household, there was a strong determination to deal with any other children who were nasty to one of the family. I remember one incident when I was called 'skinny' and my father waded into the offenders and chased them across the village. When he caught them, he lifted his trouser leg and showed them what had been hidden: his scars from the war. They soon dropped their heads and said they were sorry, even extending their apology to me.

One noticeable quality in our family was that we seemed not only to be individuals, but also to have marked similarities in personality, including all being emotionally robust and fairly intelligent. The boys went to secondary grammar schools (or in my case a new technical high school) and the girls to girls' high schools. We were a family of thinkers who did well at school. However, our aspirations were curbed because although nearly all of us would have liked to have continued on to higher education, the family couldn't afford to offer the opportunity to more than one child. John was the only one to go to college, and he then became a professor. I've sometimes wondered whether, had we been given the chance, we might have ended up as a family of professors!

Looking back at our life as children, there were certainly tough moments and some bullying, especially for the children of an ex-butler and head chef of stately homes, who both had strong views on honesty and manners. Sometimes the discipline at home was a bit strict, but we managed our crowded lives as those in large families must find a way to do. My mother showed such love that we perhaps took her for granted and were quite lazy around the house, always choosing to be outside playing and running around in nature, which was encouraged.

My mother was well organised, extremely hardworking and an archetypal mum who lived to look after and provide for her children and husband. Her daily domestic tasks were unremitting, on top of which she breast fed over an incredible time span of twenty years. Apart from having asthma, mum also suffered from Meniere's disease and was confined to bed for several days every few months. I could see her struggling whenever she was feeling ill, with the room spinning around her. To try and lessen the symptoms, she used an old wives' remedy of a bandage soaked in vinegar wrapped around her head. She was intelligent and enjoyed reading, especially if I would stand behind her and brush her beautiful, long brown hair while she read. My mother played the piano too and delighted in accompanying our singing; her favourite song was a Doris Day number called 'Secret Love'. She was the eldest of ten siblings and her parents were committed Christians as her father was a lay preacher.

With no buses running through Winterton, my mother wasn't often able to go into town; she was very much tied to village life and home. She sometimes worked as a seasonal picker in the fields, which gave us a sporadic supply of fruit and vegetables, and her customers often paid for her laundry services with the food they had grown. We cultivated a few edibles in our small garden, and there were a couple of small local shops for groceries and basics.

Mum never complained, even when there was no food in the larder and no money to buy any of the vitals for the family. Indeed, she somehow managed to provide for our every need, even down to that luxury meal of bread and dripping at least three times a week, and the bowls of tea-sop which consisted of stale homemade soda bread, hastily broken up and dropped into hot tea. We had few material possessions, and with post-war rationing, even a great family feast often still only amounted to bread and dripping. It would probably be difficult for young people today to imagine what it was like to make a whole meal out of bread, spread only with the animal fat from roasted meat, often cadged from a local rich family; but we considered it a treat worth begging for.

As I was the youngest boy in the family, Mrs Duck, who lived next door, gave me an egg each week which my mother boiled for me. With her trained precision, she would cook the egg perfectly by starting off with cold water, bringing it to the boil and simmering for exactly three minutes and twenty seconds. It always had a runny yolk and hard white, and I still use this method today! I recently discovered that Mrs Duck was a resistance agent in the war and was awarded the Legion d'Honneur.

She also won several other medals, worked bravely behind enemy lines as a soldier and translator and was responsible for many foiled German plans.

On one occasion I saw hundreds of villagers running through the village towards the sea, darting down the main road carrying bowls, saucepans, baskets, fishing nets, bags and any other receptacle they could find. A ship carrying Jaffa oranges had run aground and the cargo of oranges had been washed up on the beach, having been tipped overboard by the nervous crew as they desperately tried to lighten the vessel; though sadly to no avail. I remember how in every cubbyhole, in every outbuilding, under the stairs, around the kitchen and even in the garden, we had piles of free juicy oranges. They were usually not available to us except at Christmas, and the frequency of diarrhoea filling the thunderbox was a demonstration of how we gorged on this mouth-watering fruit without due consideration, until my dear mother curtailed our gorging. A large family could collect so much more than a small one, and we had months of lovely marmalade made by my skilful mother, the former head cook.

Suppertime was the main daily event in our home, with the entire family sitting round the small table, often alongside a couple of poor village children who regularly dropped in to sample a mouthful of the lovely sop. We always had a verse at supper and the manners my father demanded were actually quite royal, despite the meagre food on our table. If I had to describe an aristocrat by demeanour and behaviour rather than wealth, it would be my father; and a lady, my mother.

My father had many gifts which he shared with me, and because of his coaching I know how to spell almost any word in the dictionary and can handwrite beautifully. He also taught me how to present myself smartly, valet my tweeds, mend a clock, and strip and rebuild a car engine. Following his years in service in the 1920s he had many different jobs, including a spell working as a travelling salesman for a gas cooker company, which must have allowed him to make good use of his natural charm and gift with words. One of my earliest memories was of waiting for him to return home from work on his rickety old bicycle with his suit trousers clipped to his thin ankles to stop his turn-ups catching in the oily chain. My parents never owned a car and neither could drive.

My father was an immaculate dresser, a real gentleman, and it must have pained him to have to crease his trousers for the daily cycle ride to work. He seemed to ride so slowly and sedately, and his pending arrival at home after a day's work, meant the kettle would be set ready on the hob by his fond wife. My father never drank his tea out of a cup; instead he poured it into the saucer so that it cooled down and could be enjoyed quickly. He claimed that Edward VIII did the same thing, and he thought it was good form to copy royalty. I wondered whether my father served that king; or was he watching through a crack in the doorway, as the royal butler had the honour of serving his majesty?

We knew when he was likely to be coming over the hill from his work, and we competed to be the first member of the family to spot his faint silhouette in the distance. My mum was always the first to see his dark shape, and she often teased us about being able to see through to the other side of the hill as he pedalled up to the peak from the far side. Ever so occasionally a chocolate bar might appear, which he would slowly and enticingly pull from his jacket pocket for his excited children; more often than not there was just the one bar to share between all of us.


After WWII, people in the village were a very close community. There were of course a few odd bods, a grumpy man or two, the so-called village idiot and occasionally a disabled child. The children whose fathers had been in the wars, as mine had been, could easily be picked out by their fathers' injuries. Some locals, though, seemed quite nasty and one such, an ex-soldier from the trenches in WWI, lived in a black wooden hut that no one dared visit. Apparently, he used to eat children for tea and carried a gun for shooting people. He had a white beard, wore only one medal on his chest and always carried a staff.

One day in the summer of 1949, aged five, I was playing on a stone wall near his home, when I stood on a loose stone and toppled into a large patch of nettles. I was with a friend, and we both screamed so loudly that the man shot out of his house with a big stick. Seeing the situation, he poked the stick towards me, and I clung onto it as he pulled me out. He carried me into his hut while my friend ran home to tell my mother that I was in the old man's house.

My mother came running, to see this dark figure carefully carrying me in his arms and holding a bunch of dock leaves as he slowly walked towards the gate. She gazed at this strange scene, wondering what on earth was going on, and then took me and the leaves from him and carted me home. That man, called Dardler, cared for me until I left Winterton, and when I was an adult I visited him in his old age and got to know him. He was a kind, gentle and highly intelligent man who was a major in the Battle of Passchendaele and had several pieces of shrapnel in his body which he seemed to tolerate quite well. He sold his Victoria Cross in 1968 so that he could live on the proceeds as a supplement to his pension. He passed away the year after I left the army, and I was privileged to learn from him that what a human being appears to be is not necessarily who they are.

My first infant school in Winterton was housed in a charming old eighteenth century building and proved a tough challenge for an active and freedom loving five-year-old. From the school windows I could look out and see the wonderfully enticing sand dunes and sea – which didn't help me to keep my attention on the class. The teachers were strict and kept us regimented, probably typical of teachers and teaching throughout post-WWII Britain.

My keenest recollection of infant school is of being made to drink milk at break time, with one teacher holding me down whilst another forced the milk down my throat. Even the smell of the milk made me feel sick and I would cry, scream, splutter and struggle, but they persisted every day until I vomited. It was some weeks before the state would allow us to choose orange juice instead of milk, and it took a visit from my father to the school to stop me from being force-fed a food which, to no ill effect, he never drank. He informed them of something we now know – that many people are allergic to dairy products; and indeed, due to this allergy, I have never been able to consume milk, cream or butter on their own.

We had quite a strict Christian upbringing, and we all went to church throughout our childhood. The entire family would don their best clothes and walk to church on Sundays, plus we attended the special services at Christmas, Easter and Whitsun. The children went to Sunday school on Sunday afternoons, but I found it full of things I didn't understand, and there was a lot of bobbing up and down and kneeling – not overly appealing to a lively young boy!

Winterton was in a beautiful, wild, rugged area and life could be fun for a youngster living in such an unspoilt place, despite the abject hardship and extreme poverty. I had no bicycle, and an ice cream on the beach, perhaps just once in the summer, was something to look forward to; but simply playing outdoors around the village was enough to give us great joy. The rolling sand dunes, the turbulent foam-crested green sea and the coastal offshore winds all created an exciting playground. The coastline was a mass of huge concrete blocks, each over a hundred cubic feet, stretching for miles and constructed as barriers against a potential German invasion. I can still picture little Sarah Holt at eight years old, standing proudly on top of one of the blocks, pulling aside her knicker-leg and urinating onto the sand below under the gaze of the older boys who were taunting her to perform more dares.

In the late 1940s air raid shelters still lined the higher parts of the Winterton coast, and the horizon along the top of the valley was decked with Pom-Pom guns that we could whizz around on and use to play army games. I adored those guns and the shelters which echoed with our shouts and laughter as we ran around inside, and it was only as an adult that I realised what we'd been playing with. The Germans never invaded, so these defences were to become obsolete and stand as memories of what could have taken place. They remained there for more than twenty years after the Second World War, symbols of the nation's determination to protect our beautiful country at all costs.

An old BSA 500 army motorcycle left over from the war, without an engine though still with reasonable tyres, lay rusting on the top of a sand dune. We used to jump, one by one, onto the back seat as the older boys steered it down a steep sandy hill, using us little ones to help push it back up the slope again as they got ready for the next descent. It was a quick ride down and a very long push up that hill. I relished the game, but regularly fell off, although I never seemed to hurt myself; when one was having such fun, pain tended to be ignored.

Every year the local people had an adder round-up along the valley that ran from Winterton in the north, to Hemsby, about two miles to the south. Adults, followed by children, from the two villages would drive the fleeing and frightened adders towards their death, whilst men and women with long sticks beat the marram grass that grew out of the sand dunes.

When these poor hunted creatures had no escape and revealed themselves through their wriggling panic, the men would catch them with snake-catching nooses on the ends of long sticks, impale them on the thorn bushes that lined the edges of the valley and then burn the bushes. Any grass snakes caught up in the hunt could be thrown back into the grass, and I remember many small children handling them without fear. One foolish boy mistakenly chased an adder and grabbed it by the tail, to be quickly chastised by an adult. I'll never forget the snakes coming out of the grass onto the sandy pathways as they wriggled away from the oncoming beaters towards the end of the drive. I appreciate now what a cruel and heartless business it was.

This mass murder was to ensure that the snakes didn't menace the thousands of holidaymakers who thronged to the beach each summer;

it was a practice learned from soldiers stationed there in the war who were afraid of the vipers. I know today, though, that a bee sting is more dangerous than an adder bite. The last time I was bitten by an adder was with a fast strike from a large snake as I ground-baited my fishing swim, and I only suffered slight nausea plus two small holes in my leg, marked by tiny blobs of blood.

Despite the annual hunt, adders still thrived in that valley and occasionally we found them in our garden. I remember one day, as a small boy, hiding under the kitchen table from whatever our dog would bring in next. Mark, our Labrador, suddenly shot through the kitchen door with the largest adder I have ever seen wriggling in his mouth. I could see its fangs striking fiercely into Mark's fur.

Mark was the family pet, an exemplary guard dog and an affectionate and beautiful boy who, when he wasn't running around the garden, was often lying in a basket with Tiddles, our sweet cat and mouser extraordinaire. The longest adder ever caught in Britain measured over four feet eight inches, and this one must have been over four feet! My mother wrestled the snake from the dog's mouth, dispatched it with a poker and threw it into the stove. She was bitten on her wrist, though luckily there was no venom left to do any harm.

I was free to wander from a young age, and I carry in my heart and will always treasure, delightful memories of the exhilarating freedom that charged my early life. I loved to roam and to create an imaginative world in which I could live and play. When I was a boy, I was the youngest Tarzan ever! No public park, no woods or forest could be resisted, and all I needed to feel like the real Tarzan was an ape or two to be my companions. Although mindful of the difficulties faced by my large family and the struggles that life's challenges offered my parents, I thoroughly enjoyed my young life. I didn't fully resonate with the deprivation my family experienced; I was a child having fun and being free, and I thrived on this diet of play and adventure. In those times I had no real fears, and to me, all the villagers were like one big family.

# CHAPTER 2

# GREAT YARMOUTH

In 1950 my father was able to secure a job as a printer in the local town of Great Yarmouth. He sold Stone Cottage and with the proceeds bought a boarding house, about five times bigger than the old cottage which was demolished soon after we moved out. King Street was quite a closely packed street, with a ladies' hairdressers on one side of our house and a men's tailors on the other. I remember it as being a really friendly neighbourhood, though the other side of the street from our house had been bombed and was lined with derelict houses.

Yarmouth is famous for its rows, the narrow alleys that weave between the blocks of houses, many of which were built in Charles Dickens's time. Dickens wrote one of his most famous works, Oliver Twist, in a hotel on the seafront at Great Yarmouth at a time when there was great poverty. Throughout its history the town was generally poor, except for a period when it was Europe's main fishing port for herring.

Our new Yarmouth home was built in the eighteenth century and had seven bedrooms, three family rooms and a kitchen. We had open fireplaces and it was three storeys high. Each bedroom had a door, and there were even sinks in each room. Since we only had a lavatory in the back yard, we resorted to buckets in the evenings.

Carrying a bucket down three flights of steep stairs to be emptied in the outside drain meant that there was a lot of slopping. No wonder the stairs always smelled of urine and poo. I once tripped and fell, pouring the contents of the almost full bucket down two flights of stairs. I never told anyone what had happened and have kept the secret until now!

I can't remember ever using a toothbrush, and we had no bathroom, only a large, galvanised tub which hung on an outside yard wall by one of its handles. My older sisters, Joan and Kim, scrubbed me once a month, with the latest washing powder sprinkled into tepid water as a form of bubble bath. I hated the carbolic soap they used to brighten my skin. They seemed to take great pleasure in scrubbing my scrotum with a hard brush laced with carbolic, accompanied by their raucous laughter.

The new house had space, and we no longer had to squeeze in. Indeed, to supplement our income, my mother filled the place with paying visitors during the summer, and underneath the house was a large cellar that my father commandeered for his printing business as it became more successful.

Up until 1951 I'd never travelled more than a few miles, except for the trip from Hereford to Winterton, so this move to Great Yarmouth was a big adventure. Although life was still hard and challenging, with little to eat as there were eleven to feed, plus a few additional guests at our supper table. Because of rationing, there just wasn't much food. I remember the daily task of nipping down to the shops with the ration book for the daily 'pinta' and a few morsels; it was all we were allowed at the time.

After rationing ended in the mid-1950s my mother came into her own again by standing in the kitchen and doing what she did best – cooking for her family. She was a splendid and expert creator of delicious food, the skill she had learned whilst in service. Although the choice of ingredients was limited, she always managed to prepare an appetising evening meal.

In the 1950s we often ran out of money for the electric meter when my father had no shillings, so I would be sent out into the streets to ask passers-by if they could give me a shilling piece for some change; mostly what we'd gathered from behind the cushions on the settee. In those days it was half-crowns, florins, sixpenny pieces, threepenny bits, pennies, halfpennies and farthings. Some years earlier we also had groats. It sometimes took ages, yet I always seemed to succeed in bringing back a shilling, to the relief of the family.

One night my father sat us all down and said that he was fed up with us being cold and hungry. He took some copper sheeting from his workbox and fashioned over thirty shilling-sized discs which he put in the meter when we needed electricity. He filed them so accurately and carefully that each one looked like a work of art. He didn't seem to take into account that when the meter man came to empty the meter, he would be found to be embezzling power. When that time came, he pleaded with the man for time to cash in the discs for real shillings. It was heartening to live in a town where people could understand and have sympathy for what others were going through.

My father had acquired an old Adana hand-printing press, some lead type, printing ink and other bits and pieces and taught himself how to set up a small printing business. I loved working with him, and I was even allowed to compose the letterheads that he seemed to be endlessly printing for various local businesses. The type was in a large wooden case, and each letter was labelled. When I discarded what had been used, I often threw the type randomly anywhere into the type-case. The castigations I received taught me a great lesson in life which still serves me today: if a job is worth doing, it is worth doing properly.

As a self-employed printer, my father was often owed money so it behoved the youngest and spriteliest child to trip around the town and knock on the doors of those who had received printing and not yet paid. Off the mark went 'spring-heeled Jack' as I was called. I often delivered orders at night, and on cold nights I would go from house to house to ask for the money owing, which I was usually given. Who could possibly turn down a starving street urchin collecting for his wounded father? I could see why he sent his scruffy little son to call in the debts – people would take pity on me and pay up, especially when I was running around the streets during the winter months with snow coming into my well-worn shoes. I cut cardboard from our Weetabix packets into the shapes of my shoes and used them as inserts to protect against the road; though any damp soon disintegrated my flimsy insoles. My brothers and sisters and I used to fight to get to the packets first.

I can still picture my father limping down the road in search of printing jobs. He was always polite, invariably helping those less fortunate than him and forever smiling, tipping his brown trilby as he went quickly about his errands. He never spoke about his war injuries, but I knew they were serious and as he hobbled down the road, I could see his limp leg being dragged behind him – though only a little, because he could sense when I was watching. Dad's story was that he was run over by an American soldier's lorry as he lay resting by the roadside. I didn't question this tale, and it never occurred to me that I should. However, I later learned that the episode was much more perilous than he'd told us and had changed his life immeasurably.

From army boxing champion in 1928 to a limping father of nine, he must have had many untold inner challenges that I never realised until his death. On one occasion I caught a glimpse through an open bedroom door of my father bandaging something up. The procedure was done with such perfection and confident expertise that it must have been a daily act, so quickly and skilfully was it executed. He was strapping himself into the medical truss which held in his intestines. How I wish I could convey to my father now my utter respect for his courage in not wanting to receive any sympathy. Even though I have studied scores of real-life heroes as a history teacher, my dad remains my unsung hero.

From around that time, one of my father's sayings had a profound and lifelong effect on me. He used to say:

'Life is a golden chalice – go out and fill it.'

The image of the golden chalice took root in my mind and fired my imagination. I was taken with the idea that the heart of life is somehow pure and golden. Later on this notion became the luminous image that I used to refer to anything that was especially dear to me and close to my heart. It became a rich golden thread that ran through my life, always inspiring me and drawing me towards doing my best in every situation.

As I looked across the road from our house to the fallen-down houses opposite, I could see people living amongst the bricks in abject squalor and total poverty, at night displaying Hurricane lamps as their only source of light. Some had been in WWII and the majority had no opportunity to live in a house with water, a lavatory and somewhere safe to sleep. A lot of children of my age were living there and despite their difficult circumstances, they always seemed to be smiling. In the summer sun, the rows would be full of young children playing and parents sitting outside, knitting and sewing and passing the time of day. Almost every dad I saw was smoking, but I never saw a woman smoke.

One family with thirteen children stood out from the rest. As I used to walk down the rows to go shopping for my mother, I was aware of one of them – a young girl with a runny nose, dressed in rags, who was often playing the penny whistle. I could hear her playing when I was in bed, and it was such sweet music. Despite her gentle smile, Rosie Hogg looked dejected with a dirty face, greenish teeth (as many of us had back then) and a smell of rank staleness as you walked past her.

Later on at school, Rosie was shunned by the other children and was inevitably bullied and teased, yet she never cried or complained. The other girls would pull up her dress in front of the boys, revealing that she wasn't wearing any knickers. And the teachers would threaten any child who couldn't give a correct answer in a lesson with being made to sit next to Rosie Hogg. I became aware at an early age that there were children growing up in circumstances far more challenging than mine.

# CHAPTER 3

# JUNIOR SCHOOLDAYS

Soon after arriving in Great Yarmouth I was enrolled at Greenacre School on Dickens Avenue. I enjoyed junior school because I was privileged to have as my class teacher an ex-army major who fought with General Wingate in Burma, was captured and tortured by the Japanese and decorated with the Military Cross. Charlie Philips was mentioned in dispatches three times. He was a rugged man, built like a rugby player and always immaculately turned out in his brown demob suit, shiny shoes and smartly knotted regimental tie, his hair neatly combed and held in place with a liberal serving of Brylcreem. Major Philips was the person responsible for inspiring me to develop my handwriting. He taught brilliantly and I remembered what he imparted; it was a joy to have such a noble and heroic teacher.

There is usually one teacher in life who gives us hope and who can be emulated for the quality of their humanity, and Major Philips was that one teacher for me. He was the first teacher who I felt actually saw me for who I really was inside. He could see my abilities and potential, beyond the outer image of a scraggy boy in hand-me-downs from a poor background. His astuteness and understanding were life-changing for me, as up to that point I had not felt truly seen or valued by anyone outside the family. Coincidentally, his father was also a butler and his mother a chambermaid, at Petworth House in Sussex.

In contrast to the encouragement from my teacher, as a poor boy who was privileged to get free school meals, I had to claim them each week in front of everyone which felt like a routine humiliation. On Monday mornings, when all the richer pupils handed in their five shillings for school meals for the week (about 25p in today's money), there were three urchins who had to swallow their pride and ask for free meals because they were in need:

'Please sir, can I have free school meals because my mum and dad have no money?'

We three had fathers who had been in the war and perhaps as a consequence were down on their luck, or they had large families. Many still wore their demob suit, like Major Philips. We three 'urchins' are all now in our seventies and I've been able to follow the lives of the other two through the internet. George Philpott became a doctor who specialised in brain surgery and is now retired. Sarah Danby became a lawyer, retired aged sixty after a successful career at the Bar and now lives in Marseilles. I was a teacher and headteacher. All three of us have much to be thankful for; perhaps those free school meals were laced with wisdom and determination? Actually I put it down to Major Charlie Philips; what a great man.

The good thing about being poor was that the dinner ladies, who knew me well and knew my family's circumstances, always gave me a lot extra to eat. I hated bread and butter pudding, but loved the sponge and suet puddings they used to cook. Hot custard was liberally dripped onto the peaks of the puddings and ran down to mix with the jam or treacle, making my mouth water in anticipation.

One day I was tripped whilst carrying my 'spotted dick' pudding to the table, and I fell, dropping all of it onto the shoes of one of the teachers. He kicked me, slapped my head, called me a 'cretin' and then brutally ordered me to lick the custard off his shiny shoes and wipe them clean with a damp cloth supplied by the trembling dinner monitor. The dinner ladies looked on in disgust, and thank goodness I didn't have to lick his boots, because a kitchen lady arrived with a mop, just in time to save me!


Out on the streets, Jimmy Spillane, a nasty local boy whose father was a drunk, was always waiting, ready to jump on me and beat me up. He and his quarrelsome gang ensured that I'd be trembling in my bed at night, terrified of the next day's trip to the shop. I would try to find a diversion, and thinking I was being clever, would dart back home down a previously unused alley and dash through bombed buildings, only to be pounced on again. I remember the black eyes that seemed to be a permanent feature on my young white face, until one day I followed my father's instructions and planted a sharp straight right on Jimmy's nose. It bled and bled, and he cried and cried, and I never saw Jimmy Spillane again. I later learned that he had died aged only fifteen, having fallen under a lorry in the harbour area of town whilst cadging herring.

I have loved fishing since childhood, maybe partly initiated one Christmas when my mother gave me Ernest Hemingway's The Old Man and The Sea. I read it several times by candlelight and so wanted to catch a marlin, but didn't think I'd ever get the chance to even see one. One of my favourite adventures was when my mother sent me off to the herring fleets as they tied up their romantic drifters along the river's edge. There could be up to thirty boats across the river Yare, stretching from Haven Bridge to the harbour's mouth, a distance of a mile. They were literally stacked gunwale to gunwale across the river, and I could run across them to the other side of the river and back, sometimes shouted at or chased by angry captains.

Nobody seemed to care about health and safety in those days. As the drifters were being unloaded, the 'cran' baskets which were filled with fish in the hold of the boat, were swung over onto the quayside, and a few herrings always slipped off the heavily laden woven baskets. The onlooking fishermen would gesture with a look or a nod when it was alright for me and the other poor shivering young boys and girls to nip in and steal the herrings that had fallen onto the cobbled stones of the quay.

Stuffing the wet, slippery fish inside my shirt, down my trousers and anywhere I could find to conceal them in case anyone checked that I had taken more than a few, I headed home to my waiting mother. I loved her praise, and one day I deposited over twelve herrings on the kitchen table, along with a rare mackerel and a large eel!

I was also drawn towards north Norfolk, to the lifeboat station where great men had rowed the seas to help stranded sailors. Henry Blogg, thirty-eight years a coxswain, was my boyhood hero and still has a place in my heart.

Cromer, Blakeney and the villages around north Norfolk were especially appealing. Cromer was the place, and still is, of the world-renowned Cromer crabs; yummy gold-red carcasses that offer such delectable crab meat. I used to scrounge them from the 'crabbers' when they hauled their boats up the sandy beaches at Cromer, Winterton and Hemsby. They were always kind, and I never went without a crab or two. These crabbers' stamina, courage, leather-like hands and golden hearts were a comfort to a youngster, and all I wanted was to grow up to become one of those men – a man of the sea, a hard worker and a crab eater!

Sometimes I cadged a trip with a shrimper, and if I'd chosen the right skipper, I could help the crew use the scoop net or haul in the longer driftnet which sometimes caught a stray herring. It was the same with the whitebait, the sprats and anything else that could be hauled up from the murky sea. I loved those days, and the flint houses of Cromer have imprinted on me such a strong image of mathematical perfection that I sometimes drive there with my family to visit the lifeboat station and view the photographs of a hundred years past; and to wonder at the flint houses that fascinated me as a boy.

One day a huge whale was beached at Horsey. The poor animal lay floundering in the shallows and eventually died in front of a group of over a hundred frustrated onlookers. They stood helplessly on top of the sand dunes, gazing down and wondering why they couldn't muster up enough force to heave the giant leviathan back into the waves with the ropes they'd wrapped around its body. They hauled and hauled each time a wave came ashore, but to no effect.

That day we were taken out of Greenacre School and driven to Winterton in a charabanc, and when we arrived and were given the nod, we all hared down to the beach and turned towards Horsey to see the spectacle. I can still see that creature's eye as the local people pulled on the ropes, trying to get the great and beautiful whale into the sea. Alas, it was not to be. That eye, as I remember it, glowed with understanding, gratitude and great pain. One of the amazing things that warms my heart is that we can still recall such past images with extraordinary clarity and photographic detail, even from as long as seventy years ago. I think that seeing the epic battle with the whale was a great help to me in later years.

Another striking memory is of the Christmas parties given by the RAF association for disadvantaged children whose fathers had been in uniform during the war. As an invalid from the war, my father was eligible to bring all his children to these wonderful events arranged by WWI and II veterans and their wives, so that the children could experience a little of Christmas, despite their poverty.

To me as a young boy, barely eight years old, the lucky dip was the most exciting fun thing arranged at the parties, and I always chose it, flicking my small hands through the pine-smelling sawdust; was there a pot of gold in that tub? Or perhaps some gold ingots in the form of a small metal truck bearing the lettering 'Made in Hong Kong'. Or a red London bus with a key on the side that I could wind until the spring was tight and then launch across the floor whilst the other boys and girls did the same with their buses and trucks, along with a few articulated Dinky lorries for the older children. Such fun, and the toys must have only cost a few pence.

At one of these parties, a very old soldier sat beside me, and we had a conversation. He asked about my school life and family, and when I shared some elements of these with him, he looked at me through his one eye and posed this question:

'Young lad, do you think it is possible to have had a challenging upbringing and describe it as blissful?'

I know that my response at the age of eight was instrumental in forming an understanding that one can suffer hardship and yet be thankful that such hard times have helped shape one's adult life. This man, whose name was Cadger, shared a little of his story with me as he pushed a half crown into my hand.

'Take this, lad, and remember that to suffer hardship is to become a man!'

I didn't really understand this approach until later in life; but at the time I did glean some details about when he was a boy in the late nineteenth century, living in a workhouse and barely surviving the brutal conditions. I can still see the creases in his eyes as he told me. He was born in 1869, so was about eighty-four when we talked.

My mother had by this time taken in George Denton, an incontinent seventy-five-year-old retired violinist from the Halle Orchestra, Malcolm Tricker, an ex-serviceman, Ben Sanowawa from Nigeria and Freddie Luxton who was suffering from post-WWII trauma, having been tortured by the Japanese. From time to time friends of my brothers and sisters, and some of the older married siblings, were also crammed in with us. We were one big family with many in a bed, little to eat and two exceedingly hardworking heads of our extended household.

Thursday was the night that the drivers from the BDH – a big chemical company called The British Drug House – would spend the night at our house for bed, breakfast and evening meal which cost them five shillings each. I remember hanging around their table at suppertime, hoping for a stripe or two from their leftover bacon. How I yearned for those stripes! I know now why my mother gave these men such a good meal whilst we were always hungry – we desperately needed what they paid. My mother would sometimes hide the money from our boarders and visitors in between the saucepans in the kitchen in order to save it for her housekeeping, and so that my father wouldn't be tempted to spend it or generously give it away to those in need. One day when I was helping with the cooking, I inadvertently boiled up some of these hidden pound notes along with the potatoes. Luckily the notes were rescued, dried out and declared fit for use!

Both my parents were kindhearted, and my father's generosity and kindness were legendary amongst all who knew him. He would help anyone he could and constantly went out of his way to show extra kindness to everyone who crossed his path. His attitude rubbed off on me, and being kind became second nature. In spite of all my tribulations and sometimes wanting to get my own back on those who had been less than kind to me, I knew that kindness would be important in how I lived my life.

By the mid-fifties my father was working from home and only had a break once a year for an hour or so to take Christmas dinner. Christmas was, by then, a big affair with the lodgers and all the family present, including the wives and young children of those already married. It was quite a squeeze as thirty-five of us sat around our oval Georgian dining table for the festive lunch and carefully shared and then devoured all the trimmings with, unbelievably, just one large chicken between us all. But the happiness flowed, and I can still taste that bird.

Regardless of the hard times, I'm glad to have been part of my big, bustling family and was immensely fond of them. Yarmouth, though, was in some ways a dire place to live; a rather shabby seaside resort, overrun with almost a million summer visitors each year. How I always looked forward to October when the summer season drew to a close, the cod and whiting were in the waves and there was relative, although cold, peace in the town. In hindsight, I mostly loathed Yarmouth; how on earth it got the prefix 'Great' I'll never know!

The Yarmouth streets were walked by shipwrecked sailors and ex-servicemen who had lost their way and most of whom had served in WWI and some in WWII. Many lived in the big shipwrecked sailors' home on the seafront. Its inhabitants dressed in dark blue serge sailors' suits and peaked sailors' caps and wandered aimlessly, looking for dog ends that had been flicked onto the roads and pavements by those who could afford to smoke. I remember seeing one of these 'heroes' pick up a butt end and in the distance behind him was a huge poster displaying a sailor in his blue uniform with the words 'Players Please'. Players was the favourite smoke of these men, and indeed of all those who were able to buy the sweet-smelling Virginia tobacco.

These poor lonely men invariably dived on the discarded remnants of a fag and proceeded to take what was left of it and roll it with the other stubbed ends they'd gathered from the gutters, to make a smoke. I never saw a filter when I was young. It was pitiful, and I couldn't begin to imagine the deprivation they suffered. It must have been dreadful, so I forgave them their strange ways and helped them when I could.

One day I saw a man outside our house who had a loud tic, due to nerve damage from the war. He was trying to pick up a cigarette butt from the gutter, but couldn't manage it because of his violent tremors. I picked it up for him and gave it to him, and when I told my father about the man, he encouraged me to help. I remember collecting more than a dozen fag ends to give to an old sailor who had shell shock and couldn't roll it himself. I separated out the tobacco and rolled five neat, thin cigarettes, lighting the first one for him as he trembled excitedly, desperate to smoke.

This mix of brave men who had chanced their lives for their country, the shell-shocked soldiers and sailors who now had no life, was a normal part of my everyday young world. I must confess that I often crossed the road when a group of them approached, because I didn't understand and they looked menacing as they shook and stared at anyone who walked by, their piercing eyes ogling every moving shape. One could clearly pick out those who had fought, because some had lost an arm or a leg and some were partially sighted or had part of their face missing.

I remember one man who always skipped along the pavement hurriedly, with a face part-made of plastic and his one eye staring through a monocle. On closer examination, I noticed that he also had a wooden leg and his mouth was askew. His rotting teeth and balding head combined to make him look like something of an ogre. One day he dropped his cap and I picked it up carefully as I was passing. He spoke to me so kindly and eloquently through his twisted face that I felt I was being thanked by a very well-spoken angel. He was Squadron Leader Chris Calvert, an ex-Spitfire pilot and a great man who had been shot down by the Germans yet managed somehow to survive.

Many of these unfortunate, shell-shocked, shaking men could be found queueing outside the town's 'slipper baths', as they were called. In such a place, a hot bath could be bought for fourpence and it was my monthly treat to be allowed to immerse myself in the hot, deep baths and have some soap to wash and shampoo my hair. As a boy, I would often receive a discount and pay only a penny or twopence, but I had to beg and plead my case, depending on who was in charge of the baths that day.

Those baths have never been beaten and for the sake of a hot bath, I even tolerated the black scum that stuck to their sides from the men who bathed there. Later, when my older brothers were married and lived in their own council houses, I could arrange to have a bath once a month at their homes, though I had to bring a shilling for the meter to heat the water. To get to my brother Reg's house in Gorleston-on-Sea, I walked two miles each way; but I was clean and felt like a million dollars after my bath. I wonder if they ever found out that I once put a copper shilling made by my father into their meter!

At home we were all taught to be as self-sufficient as possible, and by the time I was ten I could darn socks, iron my own clothes, press my trousers, knot my tie in a number of different styles, value a used suit, warm my own bed with a bottle of hot water, clean my teeth without toothpaste using household salt, earn my own pocket money, bake bread, cook a host of meals and cover the holes in the bottom of my shoes with foot-shaped cardboard from cereal packets. I'd become a swimming spectator, and as I was living in a seaside town, I went swimming almost every day in the summer months by climbing through a hole in the pool fence. I would get changed behind a wall and go in for a dip, wearing my older brother's oversized costume. I learned to swim by watching a class of rich children and suddenly realising in my trance-like state that my feet were off the bottom – I could swim, and it had cost me nothing.

I was at that time a keen student and could write in both copperplate and cursive, well enough to get a 'Mayflower' sticker in my handwriting book almost every time it was marked. I loved learning, but I was still the underprivileged little boy who couldn't dress appropriately for school, except in hand-me-downs from my brothers and sisters that were always far too big; and I was ridiculed and teased for it.

At age ten, I won the county championships in high jump with a jump of three feet eleven inches, using the Western Roll, a style which is now out of favour. I had no spikes, jumped in bare feet and made my own shorts from a piece of grey satin that was left over from my sister's latest homemade dress.

By the time I was nearly eleven, I had been given prizes in school and was showing signs of being an athlete, winning several events at the summer sports day. I was also a chorister in the cathedral choir. The choirmaster was a dubious character, and when he asked me to come to his room in the cathedral for a chat after choir practice, his reputation was such that I ran out and never came back.

At age eleven, my spelling was fairly accurate. I remember Mrs Bunn, one of the teachers, asking for anyone in the class to name a capital city that they could spell. I put my hand up, offering 'Constantinople'. A sharp slap around the head was forthcoming, and I was reminded that it must be a capital that I could spell. I did spell it correctly; nevertheless the teacher didn't acknowledge my success.

Before I entered secondary school my handwriting was chosen, along with a few other children's, to be exhibited in front of the Queen and many educationists at an education show. It was a national exhibition of children's work throughout the land, held in London and called The British Education Show. I received some acclaim for my standard of work. Then afterwards there was a quick mention in morning assembly that Cheryl Atkinson had achieved that honour, as apparently had some young unnamed boy (me!) from the school.

My junior school excelled in two things: it was a very fine sporting and academic school, and it was also a place of incredible aggression with regular beatings – often 'six of the best' on the hand with a bamboo cane. I was absolutely terrified when I'd been found guilty of a misdemeanour and was sent to the headmaster's or second master's study for punishment. On such occasions my knees shook, and I was holding in the contents of my bowel. I would stand there terrified while Satanic Sam, as we called our headmaster, took a cane from the wall where it hung as a symbol of his power in full view of the poor wretches who were sent there.

I received not only punishment from the top – my physical education teacher resorted to violence and persecution on my bottom; a chastisement that was only meted out to boys. One day when I was sent to the headmaster's study for 'a jolly good caning' as he called it, I stood with my trousers down, waiting for the treatment I knew was coming. Alongside me, Ronnie Spilling, wearing long trousers, was urinating down his left leg with the wee filling his shoe and overflowing onto the headmaster's floor. We never knew whether or not the head noticed, or perhaps even relished, the unsavoury side effects of his reign of terror.

When I returned to my secondary school in 1974 after qualifying as a teacher, I was privy to the results that had been returned to the headmaster of Greenacre after an assessment I was given at age ten. These results were held in a file in the technical high school's archives to which I was given access, since I was the old boy tasked with organising the school reunion. I looked at the file and wondered why, as the only pupil to gain marks above 72 per cent, I was never given any praise or encouragement. The grammar school entrance pass rate was 55 per cent, but despite my high marks I was sent to the technical high school. Why did the headmaster take control of my life and deny me my rightful grammar school place? It was probably simply because poor children were not seen to belong in the grammar school.

Reading that file confirmed that I had been wrongly denied a passage to grammar school. By this time I was thirty and it was sufficient to know that I'd been good enough. Ironically, the technical high school where I ended up is now a highly successful academy school, having previously become a grammar school.

# CHAPTER 4

# LIFE AT SECONDARY SCHOOL

On the first day of term, along with the other children in their posh uniforms, I reluctantly took the school bus to Great Yarmouth Technical High School. Having passed the Eleven Plus exam in 1954 when I was ten, I was entering the school a year younger than the others, who were all eleven.

My new school was opened by the Queen in December 1953 and was a brand new, upmarket and well-equipped bastion of supposed relative normality, situated in grounds of about fifty acres. It boasted four rugby pitches, numerous sports fields, six tennis courts, a gymnasium, and full facilities, the likes of which I had not seen before nor even imagined existed. It was like a university for children.

Such schools were for rich kids, I thought. What was I doing there? The other children seemed to be so flawlessly turned out, so well shod and full of confidence. They even had packed food for morning break, neatly wrapped in greaseproof paper. These were the so-called elite of my town. Seeing their beautiful blazers with the top pocket adorned with the blue badge of a seagull and a stylish Parker 51 fountain pen clipped on, it seemed to me like I had just risen up the ranks of childhood society – whilst I still loved the old dip-pen which I'd used to write my cursive letter to the Queen. Visiting the school recently, I found that it was still like new. In hindsight, I see that this school was about as useless as a school could be; it was like a factory for children, and there was really nothing cool or excellent about it.

I was in a class of fifty-five children from a variety of backgrounds. Some came from families with money and even a car, many were from teaching families, and a good number had chosen the technical high school instead of a grammar school because of the diversity of this brand new system. As had happened at my junior school, I was placed in the D stream for the least capable pupils, since the teachers didn't imagine that a poor boy in hand-me-downs could be intelligent or academically inclined.

My dislike of this school quickly became evident, and I had many trials and tribulations there, mostly because my teachers seemed to want to hurt me all the time, slapping my head, twisting my ears, 'rulering' me, and beating me with a sharp cane. I dared not be my usual happy, exuberant self, have fun or show my natural and infectious character for fear of more harsh treatment. Even my physical education teacher, who I respected, leathered me with a plimsoll several times on the bare backside, and it stung like anything. Such sadistic events were common and made it difficult to learn, since there was a continual fear of doing something wrong.

School assembly was a time of particular trepidation, most often when the entire school was singing the school song, Servabo Fidem, and I was skylarking around and laughing to gain attention or pretend I was cool. The miscreants in my class regularly made me laugh, so being the poor boy, I was often pulled out by the collar or tie, my head slapped and ordered to report for punishment after assembly.

One evening a boy in my class poked fun at the maths teacher while he was walking along the local seafront with his wife. The next day the boy was severely punished by being caned and made to kneel in the prayer position and read the Bible in the school foyer during the morning and lunch breaks. That teacher loathed Henry and maybe disliked all boys. Henry became our hero, and we looked up to him for his courage and bravery.

Henry grew up to be a wonderful man and is now a retired JP, having served in the Royal Navy as a senior officer. I made contact with him through social media on his seventieth birthday, and we had so much to talk about. When we recalled that day of punishment, Henry told me he had died a thousand deaths as he kneeled in front of the school, and the headmaster and his class teacher had walked past, disdainfully ignoring him.

Break times at school offered the chance to join the 'in' gang and have a fag. Every boy smoked at the perimeter fence and scrounging a fag was easy. There was always one to be cadged because you would then be implicated with those who brought them to school, and therefore, if caught, you would be flogged alongside them as a partner in crime. One day I was dared to smoke in a geography lesson whilst the teacher had his back to the class. I was about to make a fool of myself when he turned round, his nose twitching and his teacher antennae erect. He walked steadily towards my desk.

'Whiting, have you been smoking?'

I responded with great courage and denied the charge. The geography store cupboard was a dark, gloomy closet where a boy and a master could easily be hidden. But nothing could muffle the shrieks as he leathered me and made me eat the remnants of the fag I'd put out and stowed in my blazer pocket. Health and Safety in the fifties? I think not!

My life in secondary school was a painful and trying time in a place of learning that I didn't enjoy. In spite of the numerous challenges, I was still able to do well in many areas. The subject prizes I was awarded were invariably slipped quietly into my hand by a teacher, either after school or in the lunch hour; whereas other winners had theirs presented on the stage during assemblies, usually to great applause. I wanted to receive a prize on the stage, and my teachers knew it. The nearest I got to that was when I was ten minutes late for school one day, having stopped on the way to cast a hand line into the river Yare to try and catch a flounder.

I was invited onto the stage, and the second master insisted I drop my trousers. With hands cupping my private parts, I bent over. Little boys like me did not wear underpants; in fact, I never wore them when I was growing up, probably because I didn't know what they were.

Bum towards the assembled school, and a single sharp crack with the stick left a red mark for all my friends and enemies to chuckle about for the rest of the week. I think I conceived the idea for The Acorn School as I walked down the steps of the school stage after that beating because it was so embarrassing to be publicly treated in such a harsh manner.

When I was being physically chastised, I had no voice, no human rights and couldn't advocate for myself. So I lay awake for years worrying about the brutality and harshness at school and dreaming of the kind of school I would create if I had the chance. It would be a place where children would be seen and encouraged to flourish for who they really were, with no harsh discipline, no detention, no being shouted at and no being sent out of lessons for behaviour that was just a natural part of a child's development. In my head, this mythical school became associated with the golden idea that had come from my father – my school would be a golden chalice! But I knew I had no chance of ever doing it. With fourpence in my pocket, those were wild and unreal dreams, said my brothers, and I dared not tell them to my friends or teachers.

When asked once by my class teacher what I wanted to do when I left school, I replied that I wanted to be a teacher, and he laughed in my face. I then said I wanted to be a doctor, and he laughed even more. His attitude was to change my life from that moment on:

'Whiting, you will never be a teacher or a doctor, so get it out of your head. The only thing you will be known for is as someone who takes up space!'

Living in the Great Yarmouth house with the lodgers and the other siblings, even though some had already left home, it was difficult to find a space to study or do the homework which was essential for a student attending such a supposedly prestigious school. And with the constant teasing from my brother, Michael, I was often disheartened and fell behind with school assignments. Mick, as we called him, used to pay me a shilling to leave the front room so that he and his girlfriend, Wendy, could be alone, presumably snogging. Doing homework by candlelight was a major task and almost impossible.

My homework was, therefore, often not completed, especially while Mick teased me and called me a college boy. Although, I suppose it wasn't a particularly unpleasant name to be called, rightly indicating as it did, that I had a keen desire to learn. I remember reading Black's Medical Dictionary and Grey's Anatomy late at night, using a self-made torch that consisted of a piece of wood on which I'd mounted a battery and a bulb in a holder. Loose wires would be touched onto the relevant terminals to get a light, the discovery of which was a real eureka moment. I read and memorised so much and had aspirations to be a doctor. I was certain by the age of twelve that I could carry out a tracheotomy, but thought I would probably struggle with a heart transplant!

When I was thirteen I went to live for a while with my oldest sister, Joan, and her family in their bungalow back at Winterton. I think this was arranged to give me a break from Mick and David's constant teasing and bullying. Mick, six years older than me, and David, three years above me, were both Teddy Boys. Popular and smartly turned out with many friends, they seemed to relish putting their little brother down as often as possible. David and I didn't have much in common, belonging to different friendship groups; he was a lot more confident than me and definitely Mr Cool. He was an intelligent student, but didn't realise his academic potential because he fell in love with quayside cranes and learned to drive them so he could take a job as a crane driver on the quayside of the River Yare as soon as he left school. Mick was a real tearaway, wearing the most highly tailored Teddy Boy suits and running around with the hard gangs. This meant that 'Cruiser Mick' was continually in fights in the local pubs and dance halls and was well known throughout the town. He loved the girls, was a heavy smoker, a keen Elvis fan and a great dancer. By the time he was twenty and I was still only fourteen, I no longer saw him that often, as he had already married and left home.

During my school years, I was often hounded because of my poverty and for having nothing material except my aluminium pencil sharpener. I loved that sharpener! Billy Shipman was the worst of my attackers; a fat and lethargic boy who I quietly referred to as Billy Bunter. He loved to spit in my ear and punch me, so when I arrived at school my first task was to dodge him and his gang, which I only sometimes managed. Billy would encourage his gang members to hold me down on the ground by offering them a penny chew. With my head forced down, he would dribble green phlegm from his disgusting mouth into my upwards-facing ear. This caused me to run to the drink fountain to try to rinse my ear out, although I never managed to flush out all the filth. He tormented me for many years, and the teachers never addressed it. My father and mother didn't ever visit my school and were unaware of what was happening.

At that time I was called 'Skinny Whiting' because my teacher said that if I stood sideways, he would mark me absent. I was very thin and malnourished and actually a bit of a gibbering wreck. Though to put this in context, practically all the children were relatively lean, and I can only remember three or four in the whole school who were obese.

Even though I'd been given a plastic bus pass, I walked the four miles to school each day, because I was so intimidated by the 'privileged' children on the bus on that first day of school, that I dared not catch it again. I'd been teased for having cold toast and marmalade wrapped in a brown paper bag, rolled into my pocket for break, and one boy had vilified me for being 'the son of a cripple'. But it was such a pleasant experience to walk to school through lovely countryside, crossing the river Yare on the ferry rowed by an old salt, that I didn't really mind.

When I was at school, bullying was somewhat divided into classes of children who would be bullied and specific groups who suffered almost constant unkindness and ill treatment. The better-off children felt they were the superior upper-class contingent, with those from hard-up families being the ones who deserved to be looked down on. Physical harassment was only between the boys. The girls were admired and fancied, so any trouble that took place between the girls was verbal or in the form of passed notes. I never saw a cat fight between the girls. However, poor and shabbily dressed girls like Rosie Hogg were very badly treated at school both by the staff and the other pupils. We took the same route home, and just for walking near to her, I was teased by my friends with chants of:

'You love Rosie Hogg. You love Rosie Hogg. You're goin' to marry 'er!'

Unbeknown to us then, there was to be another chapter in Rosie Hogg's story. When we had our school reunion as thirty-year-olds in 1974, I was the organiser and it was a grand do with formal dress, live music, a sumptuous dinner and the works. Only five of our class couldn't make it, so it was quite a gathering, including doctors, lawyers, soldiers, business people, nurses, plumbers, builders and other tradespeople. Many of the old boys and girls had done well and even the few teachers who were there seemed to be less aggressive and very different from how they'd been as our teachers.

A few from my class were gossiping and one of them said,

'I note that smelly isn't here.'

There were giggles and a few others joined the gossiping group, but I had no idea who 'smelly' was. I made the speech that was obligatory at such events, and when I mentioned Rosie, who hadn't been able to attend, there was much camouflaged tittering. At the end of the evening I was standing outside saying goodbye to everyone, when I saw a stunningly beautiful woman wearing an expensive ball gown with Italian leather shoes and highly coiffed hair. I didn't know her, so assumed she was the wife of one of the old boys. She was about to get into a silver Mercedes with her husband when I walked over and asked the man who he was, in order to tick him off on my register of attendees. He said,

'I'm Dr Philip Monroe and I'm a GP. This is my wife. She went to this school in the 1950s.'

I apologised for not honouring or even recognising his wife and asked her her name.

'Don't you remember me? I lived opposite you in King Street. I'm Rosie Hogg.'

I was absolutely stunned and a little embarrassed, so I asked Rosie what had happened to her after she'd left school at age fifteen. She told me it was quite a story. She'd managed to get a job as an office extra in London and later was given a post as a fashion adviser with Givenchy in Paris. She'd met Philip walking round the Musee D'Orsay when he was a newly qualified doctor, as they both loved art. Many of our old class overheard this conversation, and I got some letters from them the following week, commenting on the beautiful lady who, as a child, used to live in a bombed-out house.


Back in my schooldays, as the small 'Skinny Whiting' I was frightened of the local thugs, not only at school, but also in the town. There seemed to be so many young people who became Teddy Boys and liked to show their hardness. I lost count of the number of times I was physically assaulted, and except for one or two occasions, I didn't fight back.

I rather felt that it was normal to be harassed if you were poor and if your father could do nothing about it. However, that was not always so. My father once waded into a group of more than thirty Teddy Boys who were wielding their metal combs, threatening me across the street from my house because Marylou was my girl and one of the group was after her. Although my father was a small man, the group scattered like galloping horses, and they never picked on me again.

Whenever possible, the six Whiting brothers looked after one another, and when one was targeted, the others supported him if the victim dared to reveal the names of his persecutors, and if they could be caught. As a family of six boys, we were something of a group not to be messed with, and it was widely known that my father made each of us stand alone and take care of ourselves; which is why our living room became a boxing ring throughout our teenage years.

When I became an army cadet at age eleven, we used the sand dunes back at Winterton for our manoeuvres. We ran around the dunes at night, firing blanks at our army cadet friends who were playing the enemy and pretending to prepare for being real soldiers when we reached eighteen. We all thought there was another war pending. I looked forward to those night exercises: the flash from the rifle muzzles, the smell of the cordite and the crack of the blanks as we fired at each other with our old WWII Lee Enfield Mark 4s, often at point blank range. I've wondered whether such activities stayed lodged inside me, ready to be released when I was old enough to become a soldier.

We were taken there by our company commander, a twisted man who was in the SAS in the war and who was decorated for action in Germany. He often offered to drive boys home in his 1945 Ford Prefect after making sure that selected boys stayed behind to clean up and sort the weapons. A ride in a car was an unusual event for youngsters from families with no car, but the older cadets steered us away from him and protected the young ones as well as they could.

On one occasion, when I was thirteen, I had to sweep the drill hall floor after dismantling and cleaning six Bren machine guns and putting them in the armoury, so I was the last to leave, along with the officer. Despite living only three hundred yards away from the drill hall, he offered me a lift. I sat shaking in the front seat on a cold winter's evening, wondering if I would be safe. After only a few yards, Trevor, one of the cadets who had left just before I did, thumbed a lift and was picked up at the officer's suggestion. So I got out and walked home.

The following drill night, Trevor failed to attend and wasn't seen there again. In later years when we were men serving in the army, Trevor told us the story of how he was molested on the way home by this man. The details were never made public, and despite his father protesting and going to the police, no further action was taken.

I was also drawn to sports and became a competitive athlete. In 1958 at the age of fourteen, I was proud to be selected to compete for my town in a number of county events. I won first place in the high jump in the county championships, and in June 1959 I jumped five feet six inches, using the Western Roll style. I went on to achieve a jump of six feet before leaving school, and as captain of athletics I became a multi-event athlete. This skill with athletics led me to take part competitively when I was later in the British Army as well as to compete for various athletic clubs – Aldershot, Woking and Chichester. By the time I was twenty-three, I was too heavy to focus only on jumping and so became a decathlete specialising in the discus and javelin. I competed at club meets, being able to run 100 yards in 10.3 seconds, perform a decent high jump and throw the discus over 150 feet.

I was so taken with gymnastics at school that I once walked around a dance floor in a handstand, holding onto the necks of two wine bottles – a walk of over 20 metres. I could perform a standing back flip and a standing back somersault on mats and grass. I particularly enjoyed tumbling, and had I not chosen to grow so huge when I was a soldier, I could possibly have made it as a competitive gymnast. The joys of the gymnasium enthralled me, and when I returned to my school in 2016, aged seventy-two, I was pleased to see that the old gymnasium was still there, enhanced by some new equipment but with the same old beams, springboard and coconut mats; a tribute to what was probably the county's most successful gymnastics club. I had also joined the Great Yarmouth Physical Culture Club when I was eight, where I was taught and inspired by a PTI called Ernie, an ex-SAS officer who sported the Military Cross and Bar from the Second World War.

I fenced at school and was instructed by the great Kenneth Lamming, a fencer of some repute. The French names for the moves fascinated me, and I could perform a good Flèche. I began to win tournaments and regularly attended the after-school club for free as my family had no money for such things, even though it meant that I had to walk the four miles home in the dark during the cold months of winter, contemplating the many hazards. It was too dark for the ferry, so I would walk much further along the river and over Haven Bridge. Later on, I fenced in the army and was selected to compete both on the strength of my school fencing team reputation and for my performance in that skill as a physical training instructor (PTI). It was apt that my PTI badge displayed the crossed swords.

Overall, though, school became more and more of a challenge, the older I got. I was even dragged into the school choir and dressed in a cassock, which I hated. My choirmaster was deserving of a medal as he managed to cultivate in me 'the voice of an angel' – or so he said! I was a boy soprano in the early stages of my time in the choir, but was ditched when my voice broke; which was a pity as I had aspirations to become a singer. Church choirs were not really for me, as I was often slapped around the head if I didn't reach the optimum note and was sometimes made to clear up after our practices, perhaps because I stood out from the Norwich boys. I did sing, however, in the choir at Norwich Cathedral during the Christmas of 1957.

When I was twelve, my Saturday task was to collect rags and bones with an old two-wheeled cart which I pulled around the town. I could make about two shillings on a Saturday, and I was very pleased to earn that sum. At thirteen I also had a couple of jobs to support my fishing craze. When I was not ragging and boning, I took a job as a bread roundsman, peddling a black bike with a front cradle holding a big basket full of fresh cobs. The four-hour morning brought me in six shillings – about 30p in today's money.

My second job was as a delivery boy on the same kind of bike, peddling around town to deliver people's weekly orders. My bosses, the Greengrass twins, were good people and they paid me well with eight shillings for four afternoons work; about a shilling an hour or 5p in today's money.

One of my regular tasks was to deliver a huge load of shopping to the local nunnery and there was always a bag of mixed chocolate sweets called Lucky Numbers on top of the groceries. One day I opened the packet and peeked in at one of those delicious-looking and irresistible chocolates – after which I couldn't wait to deliver my next load to the sisters. Week by week I stole more and more, and one December, Mother Superior gave me a half-pound bag for Christmas. As she handed it to me, she whispered,

'I know you like Lucky Numbers!'

As Yarmouth was a holidaymakers' town, thousands of people arrived at the train and bus stations, so it was easy to persuade some of them to hire a young lad who offered to carry their cases to lodgings or wherever. By working all day it was possible to make a quick killing, carrying for those travelling to and from the resort. One day I even got half-a-crown from an elegant lady, and sometimes my takings for the day would exceed £5, a sum equivalent to my father's weekly wage in 1950. I always gave my parents three-quarters of what I earned and then divided my share in two, giving half to the shipwrecked sailors' home on the seafront. I also developed a fascination for buying things from the local army surplus store.

I once constructed a buggy that could transport large quantities of baggage, hoping that the richer ladies and gentlemen arriving at the charabanc and train stations would ask me to take them to their hotels. The Carlton Hotel was clearly for the wealthy, and I delivered countless buggies of cases and bags there. My highest tip was over one pound and five shillings from Hank Marvin of The Shadows pop group.

When I was fourteen I used the proceeds from my part-time jobs to buy my first racing cycle from Halfords. It was painted bright yellow and black, had eight gears and cost two pounds eight shillings and sixpence on hire purchase. It lasted me until I joined the army three years later. I was an enthusiastic cyclist and loved to cycle energetically through the Norfolk countryside, feeling the air whizzing through my hair, confident and rejoicing that I was so free. One day I cycled from Great Yarmouth to Norwich and back, a distance of fifty miles, in four hours.

Almost all cars back then were black, and cycling was easy as the cars travelled slowly and there weren't many of them. I first saw a white car in 1956, a beautiful Ford Cortina. I so wanted one and was eventually able to fulfil that dream when I was in the army.

In those days our entire family lived on about £5 a week, and we were continually in debt. Some weeks, my mother was unable to pay the grocery bill so she scraped and paid when she could, effectively instituting a 'Yarmouth tick'. She seemed to do without sleep and even took an evening night shift at Erie Resistor, making electrical components in their factory and coming home at ten o'clock in the evening, exhausted yet still managing to smile.

When times were tough and the winters were cold, we used to huddle around a small coal fire in the living room which was our only form of heating. We rarely had enough clothing to keep warm, and huddling was a favourite occupation of mine; or blowing my hot breath inside my clothes to feel the warmth of the air – the nearest thing to a hair drier.

During a particularly cold winter, at night when there was snow and ice on the ground and the streets were slippery and silent, my mother would send me and my brother out on an unusual errand. Taking my sister's pram, we would head to the local Beach railway station with a plan to misappropriate coal from the large piles inside the station walls. I had to shin up the high wall and jump onto the pile, and when all was quiet I would begin tossing coal over the big wall to my waiting brother who threw the pieces into the pram. When it was full, he would shout and I'd nip back over the wall.

We'd then cover the coal, placing a doll under a tiny quilt on top of our hoard, and head for home. We got away with this many times, but I was certain that one day we would get caught, and I thought we'd go to boys' prison.

One night, as we ran with the pram, we could see a large policeman standing on the snowy pavement some way ahead, hands behind his back and bobbing up and down as bobbies often did in those days. When he stopped us and asked why two young boys were pushing a large pram with a lovely dolly asleep in it, we expected the worst. Police Constable Lovell knew our family well, and when he peered into the pram and tickled the chin of the doll, the tension was absolutely unbearable.

'Off with you!' he said, and we sped home to present our mother with the spoils of our night's work. That night, in case Constable Lovell came back later, we lit a huge fire that warmed the entire house, so eager was my mother to use up our haul before there was a knock at the door; fortunately the knock never came.

At the time, I truly never thought I was hard done by, because it was all so normal, especially for those of us from a large family. With my boyhood fitness, natural ebullience, and a confidence born of surviving all that pummelling from the school bullies, I was set to rule the world. And after all, I had a yellow and black racing bike!

From the proceeds of my odd jobs, I was also able to buy the black Tommy Steele guitar that I'd seen shining like a star in the window of the local music shop. It was expensive at six pounds ten shillings, a sum that would feed a family of eleven for a week – but more than worth it to me. For a while I disappeared from the streets where everyone gathered, and gangs hung around on street corners, armed with knives and razors, ready for anyone who was looking for a fight. In the early 1950s one could rarely go about one's business during the hours of darkness without a thug challenging your right to walk the streets and wanting to engage in some form of combat.

I was at home, busy learning how to play my new instrument from a Bert Weedon do-it-yourself booklet, and as soon as I could make it through 'The House of the Rising Sun', I entered the town's music contest at The Penrice Arms. With my strong voice and three chords strummed on my new guitar, I blew the audience sky high and received a standing ovation – probably partly because the adults knew I was a self-taught, shy performer and came from a large, struggling family. On the front row sat a dozen or so scowling thugs in their long jackets and blue suede beetle crushers, manspreading with legs wide apart and combs in their hands, ready to restyle their hair if the door opened and blew it out of place. I recognised them as a tough gang that I was afraid of and who I often encountered on the streets; they looked down on me as a wimp because I didn't carry a knife or any other weapon.

Sitting in their midst was the gang's leader, Tony, one of the main street villains, known by his sycophantic servants as 'the hard man'; a thief, liar and rascal who tucked a cut-throat razor behind the castellated false handkerchief in his top pocket, ready to be drawn if anyone met his eye for a moment too long. He frowned at me and I knew he objected to my success in the contest. I took a bow after the huge applause and sat down with my older brothers and sisters where I felt safe, happy that I'd been a hit.

But later that evening I discovered that my new guitar was missing, and none of my family had seen it taken. I thought I might have carried it with me to the lavatory as I hadn't want to lose sight of it, so I went to check. And there it was, lying smashed on the floor with the strings cut. I was devastated and in tears. After the event ended, I followed a hunch and went looking for Tony, who I found outside in the street, surrounded by his laughing cronies. I bravely asked Tony if he had seen my guitar.

'Where's the little boy's guitar, then? Where is baby Elvis's guitar, then?' asked Tony in a mocking voice.

I stepped towards the thug and without hesitation, punched him on the nose, knocking him backwards. I leapt on him as he fell and punched him again in the teeth, followed by a left and right hook to the chin. I wanted to make sure I was never afraid of Tony again. Blood spilled and I got up and walked away – all seven bony stones of me. From that evening I walked the streets with a new pride and was never bothered by Tony again. In fact I didn't see him anywhere and the gang disintegrated. For a short while I was the hero of the moment and received some acclaim, plus Tony's gang members arranged a collection and bought me a new guitar for £8, a small fortune in those days.

Many years later I attempted to find out what had happened to Tony and how he'd fared in life. Eventually, in 2017, I was able to locate him through school friends and sent him a message. A year afterwards I heard back from a new and surprisingly kind Tony. He had been a probation officer for almost fifty years! Tony and I are now friends on social media and chatting with him has reminded me how important it is to forgive and forget.

Towards the end of my schooldays, in 1960, my year was given the chance to travel to Rome for two weeks to visit the Olympic Games. I was so excited, and as captain of athletics, I really wanted to go. However, it was not to be.

When the application forms were due to be handed in to the school office after parents had filled them in, there wasn't one for me. I don't think my parents were sent a form, because it never came up in conversation at home. Perhaps my teachers knew that we couldn't possibly afford the cost.

I stood in assembly and listened to the list of fortunates whose parents had been able to afford the £20 for the trip, which included a coach from school, the flight to Rome and all other expenses. The maximum amount of spending money allowed was no more than £2 per child which equalled nearly half of my father's weekly income in the 1950s.

When the group left the school in July, heading for Rome, I and three other boys were allowed to come to the school and wave them off. I actually felt privileged and never once thought that I'd missed out as it was certainly not within my parents' means to afford such a trip.

Later, in 1964, I stopped off in Rome on the way back from active service in the Middle East and stood in the centre of the Rome Olympic Stadium, quietly appreciating where I was and slowly turning around to view the great Olympic expanse. I was completely overwhelmed.

I walked to the jumping pits, sand in those days, and jogged round the track. I imagined Lyn Davies taking his three long jumps. I felt so at home and wanted to do a sub-60-second lap in my army uniform, so I went to the starting point. I set my army-issued wristwatch and ran like the wind to run the lap in 59 seconds. Wow – I had actually broken the one-minute barrier on the track used for the 1960 Olympic Games!

I dropped to the ground, panting hard because I hadn't warmed up for fear that an Italian official might stop my antics; but I had run in the Rome Olympic Stadium. And in 1965 I competed in that stadium for real, in the BAOR (British Army of the Rhine) athletics championships.

Thinking about boyhood friendships, my mind wanders back to the days when I was a young teenager and to those who were in my group. The local sandwich bar on Regent Road in Great Yarmouth was where my friends and I headed every day after school to listen to the latest rock music on the jukebox. A shilling, 5p in today's money, could play three records, and it was usually something by Elvis, Buddy Holly, The Shirelles, Adam Faith, Cliff Richard, The Everly Brothers or Billy Fury. We sat, talked and sipped frothy coffee, happy to be young people together. When we'd all been served, Ian Boon would roar up on his classy Ariel Huntmaster 500 motorbike, cockily drop it on its side stand and enter, big black gloves covering his hands and pound notes bulging out of his pockets; a great character and friend to us all, who we admired. He rode his bike well, and sometimes I would ride pillion with him.

I seemed to have few close friends at school. The one I remember with the greatest fondness was my best friend, Colin Burns, who I called Burnie. He was the son of an ex-paratrooper who had become a Norfolk farmer. Colin was the boy I identified with more than the others because, like me, he was a country boy and intelligent, but also rather smart and suave. He was a real nature lover and appreciated the beauty of the marshland surrounding his family home in Caister-on-Sea. Colin's family were like second parents to me; they always made me feel welcome and gave me a great time whenever I went to their home. I loved visiting their house and farm, climbing trees, shooting rats in the chicken run and wandering with Colin across the beautiful marshes with an air rifle tucked under my arm.

Colin's love for the beauty of all creatures served me well as it chimed with my own feelings about the natural world. He was as good a chum as one could ever find and my childhood was enriched by his friendship. With his pleasant demeanour, he was a confident and cool young boy who everybody liked. Together, we fished, hunted, played, bird-watched in the breathtaking Norfolk countryside, and generally got up to mischief on our many outdoor adventures.

Coypu, huge South American rodents that can weigh over 20 lbs, were bred for their fur coats on a nearby farm. A number had escaped to seek a new home in the marshes and had to be wiped out as they'd overrun the countryside. We would hunt them at night by torchlight, aiming our spears across the dykes and hoping to get the sixpence rising to a shilling that was on offer for each tail collected. I delighted in the marshes, the dykes, the magnificent wildlife and the fun we had riding Colin's tiny old scooter at hair-raising speeds down the country paths. My first motorcycle ride was with Colin, and I lived for those rides. Perhaps it was these early adrenaline rushes that later propelled me towards riding motorcycles in the Royal Military Police Motorcycle Display Team.

Like me, Colin loved art, and his style was expressionist. He is now a celebrated artist of international renown, and I'm inspired by his outstanding paintings of sporting and natural history and the Norfolk landscape. I experienced Colin's emerging creativity when we were studying for the A-level art exam, and we painted together at school and sketched in the marshes, drawing the captivating scenery around his house.

My friendships also extended to dancing at the local dance halls, pursuing and charming lots of lovely girls and persuading them to dance with me. Apart from the bullies, I seem to have been brought up with many lovely young people; but my closest and most rewarding friendship was definitely with Colin.

My three oldest brothers, Bill (William), John and Reg, featured in different ways throughout my childhood and teenage years and our relationships perhaps partly reflected the different age gaps. All three had gone to Paston Grammar School and were scholars with some gentle rivalry between them – Bill the poet and sailor, John the intellectual and scientist, and Reg the mathematician.

Bill, the oldest, was a smart ex-sailor, always immaculately dressed and taking his cue from my father in striving for the best Brylcreemed hair and the sharpest trouser creases. My admiration for Bill was immense and as the youngest boy, I looked up to him with some awe and devotion. He was kind and helpful and often thrilled me with stories about what it was like to be a sailor during the last couple of years of WWII. One thing he impressed on me was his anger at the encouragement the navy gave everyone to smoke until they couldn't last even a few minutes without lighting up. I learned from Bill, when he was later coughing in his thirties, that this was a downward slope, so I smoked my last cigarette when I was about twenty.

Bill was a competent mechanic, especially with motorbikes, and he was known for his collection. He maintained them meticulously and would only ride when it wasn't raining in order to keep his machines in pristine condition. After we moved to Yarmouth, he let me help him clean his bikes and would take me out riding pillion on Sunday mornings. I loved being on the motorbike out in the Norfolk countryside with my hero, Bill, who would be flaunting his unique style – a shining hand-painted helmet, polished black gauntlets and a large riding suit previously used by an army despatch rider. I really wanted my own bike and when I was sixteen, I bought myself a BSA Bantam 175cc two-stroke motorcycle from my brother-in-law for £35. It was my dream machine, and I'd learned everything I needed to know about motorbikes from Bill.

John, the second oldest, was an inspiration to me when I was at school as he was a qualified teacher of physical education and a man of many talents. It was John who I tried hard to emulate, but emulating is not always an easy road to travel. John took little notice of me when I was growing up, since at age eighteen he joined the Royal Air Force to do his national service, and straight after that he won a place at Loughborough College to study for a Diploma in Physical Education.

During my early years, Reg was a soldier in the Royal Horse Artillery, and I saw little of him. Reg had a close friendship with David, three years older than me, while I most strongly identified with Bill. During the fifties Reg worked in a bank and then in a legal practice, all the while volunteering in the Civil Defence and constantly helping people. He was a keen snooker player and loved cars. As a young man, he often seemed a rather grumpy older brother, and we had little connection until later when I was an adult.

# CHAPTER 5

# YOUNG LOVE AND WORK

When I was at the high school I fell in love with Marylou, a stunningly beautiful girl with whom I danced the dances of the time; mostly rock and roll with some additional daring gymnastic moves that we created. Marylou was my childhood sweetheart, and we went everywhere together. We danced whenever we could, even at school during break times, mostly to Elvis Presley, Buddy Holly and Bill Haley and the Comets.

Most evenings a group of us would meet in the homes of the more affluent families and create fantastic dance parties – though in those days the most we would get up to was a fag and a Vimto (a soft fruit drink). We were all in pairs and there was a sweet closeness between us. Marylou's clear blue eyes and long blonde hair tied in a ponytail, her unbelievable dancing skills, and her closeness as a girlfriend were more than a fitting accompaniment to my precious yellow racing cycle. However, compared to my bike, I'd say Marylou definitely won the day!

My younger sister and best friend throughout childhood, Dawn, mixed with my friends and was very close to Marylou. We had a lot in common, danced together and had fun. I greatly appreciated what a sensible teenager she was, holding her head high and learning how to conduct herself from our parents' Christian values and steady parenting. Dawn was the apple of their eye and had grown up into a lovely young woman.

Marylou and I became distant when I later joined the army, and I had scant news of her from friends back home. I think it was difficult for her when I moved on into the wider world. The most we did in our three years together was to kiss and hold hands, but those kisses seemed to last for hours. Such times with Marylou were a great support to me as I struggled at secondary school. But boy, could I dance! We once raised money for shipwrecked sailors by taking part in a four-hour rock and roll dance-athlon on Yarmouth beach.

In the evenings I'd also studied for two years part time at Great Yarmouth Art College and was awarded a Diploma in Fine Art. After leaving school at age seventeen, I found a job as a graphic artist in the Town Planning Department at Great Yarmouth Town Hall. I would travel to the office each morning in my three-piece suit and highly polished shoes, feeling I was about to rule the world of graphics.

During those early working days, I spent a lot of time with my good friend, Terry Whittaker. His father allowed me to drive his Morris Oxford Isis once I'd passed my test, and we had many adventures together. I particularly remember one evening in late November when I drove Terry to a dance in Norwich. I hadn't been taught to appreciate the dangers of driving on ice, and in those days salt wasn't spread on the roads, only sand from the beach – so one either had to take a chance or not drive.

Approaching Norwich Castle down Castle Street at about eight in the evening, I lost control on the ice as I drove over the top of the hill. I instinctively slammed on the brakes, and the wheels locked. If there had been a Viennese waltz playing, it would have been an incredible sight to witness as we slipped down the steep hill, twisting and turning, me wrestling with the steering wheel as I tried to master the sudden slide. The car spun round and round as though we were on a merry-go-round, and after slithering over 200 metres, we landed against the curb, luckily with no damage to either us or the car. We then crawled the almost twenty miles home in sub-zero temperatures. Within three months I had passed my Advanced Driving test and had been taught how to drive in freezing conditions.

For many years from when I was a teenager until his death in the 1980s, Harry 'Triggler' Skoyles was an important figure in my life and a mentor to me as a junior angler. Fishing was the main love of my young life, but I wasn't very good at it. I'd head off to Crossman's Lake with my self-made bamboo fishing rod, home-bred maggots and Nottingham reel built by my father, hoping to catch a monster carp.

My father was encouraging and offered me some advice with this rhyme:

> When the wind's in the west the fish bite best.
> When the wind's in the east the fish bite the least.
> When the wind's in the north the fisher goes not forth.
> When the wind's in the south the bait will fall into the fish's mouth.

At the beginning of my love affair with fishing, I only managed to catch the occasional tiny perch. One night I noticed a man fishing along the bank from me, whose rod kept bending and flexing as he caught fish after large fish. I saw that he pulled each fish over his landing net and took more time than usual to admire it before gently feeling for the hook, unhooking the animal and respectfully and carefully sliding it back into the lake. I watched him for a time and tried to emulate his style. After a while he called me over to fish alongside him, suggesting that I could cast near his float in the hope of catching more fish. Triggler caught many fish and treated each capture with the same respect. But try as I might, I could only get tiny bites and pull in little roach and perch.

Triggler kindly gave me some of the balls of paste he was using as bait. I got some bites but no fish, and at the end of the day I ran home to ask my father what was the secret of hooking a fish when it bites. And to ask my mother for some flour, dough and breadcrumbs to make bait like Triggler's.

Triggler Skoyles was the most pleasant and amiable of anglers; a legendary fisherman of great class, skill and kindness, who was prepared to help a young boy with nothing and encourage him to respect nature and the animal kingdom. I fished by his side many times, often after having ridden my yellow Raleigh bike to the lake at breakneck speed. I was always keen to see whether Triggler was fishing there, and he was my mentor, teaching me all I know about fishing. He stressed that you needed to be 'at one' with the fish, using your imagination even though you couldn't see them in the water. Triggler was so often at the lake that I even wondered whether he slept there.

One day after a long fight with a big carp I saw him draw it over his landing net and reach down, unhook it and free it back into the lake without even picking it up. I asked him why he hadn't taken the carp out of the net to look at it more closely.

'Ah, you see son, nature gave that beautiful fish to me that I was privileged to catch. And when God sends such a creature to your hook it's only right that it's not harmed and returned to its watery home with respect and thanks.'

'But why catch it in the first place?' I asked.

Triggler pulled in his rod, sat smoking his pipe and began to tell me why he fished alone, except for with me, and why he loved to catch fish and return them.

'Well, young man, that carp's weight could only be estimated by what it felt like, how hard it tugged and fought for freedom. And besides it's not about weight, it's about the challenge, the joy, the anticipation and the fact that I'm sitting by a lake in the beautiful countryside with a westerly breeze on my face, listening to a green woodpecker hammering the bark of an oak tree and seeing a kestrel swooping on a crow in the distance. Catching a fish is an added bonus, and the reason I always catch is because I have a magic ingredient pressed into my bait. That's why you only catch tiddlers, my boy; you need a magic bait! Ha ha!'

I fished the lake until my mid-twenties and caught some fish, though never as big as the ones Triggler regularly caught. Each time I went back to Norfolk to see my family, I would spend a few days fishing with Triggler, and we became very good friends; I loved his manner, his respect and his friendship. It was strange that I never saw him arrive at the lake; he was always there when I arrived, and I never saw him leave either. At times of difficulty in my life, Triggler was a great comfort to me, showing immense kindness and sympathy.

For some years I didn't realise that he was blind, until I saw a white stick lying next to his gear. I was shocked but said nothing – Triggler didn't need his eyes to be a great fisherman. The last time I saw him, I helped him up and offered to guide him to his house, which was a mile away across the fields; but he declined, saying that he'd walked home so many times he knew the way better than anyone who could see.

Sadly in 1961, when I was seventeen, and Dawn, David and I were the only siblings still living at home, my mother suddenly died in hospital from a blood clot on the brain, soon after a relatively straightforward hysterectomy. To add to the family's intense heartbreak and pain, we suspected that her death was due to post-operative neglect and therefore needless; but there was nothing we could prove.

The night we lost her, I was lying in my bedroom thinking about my mother and how lonely she must be in her hospital bed missing her nine children, when my father came into the room and gently whispered in my ear,

'Your mum is resting in heaven now,' and he kissed me on the forehead.

He must have said the same thing to the entire family, and each time he spoke, it would have been breaking his heart. He loved my mother immensely and knew how dearly we loved her too. The next evening was most awful and painful for all of us, with the entire family assembled downstairs. The wailing and crying were hard to bear, and in the background, some hours later after my father suggested we should put on some music for the young ones, Adam Faith was singing 'Love hurts'. Heaven must have been happy to receive my wonderful mother!

My oldest sister, Joan, came back, and with typical dedication she stayed in the house for a while to lovingly look after my father and those of us still at home. My mother's unfailing devotion took care of us all until the very last. Due to her prudence with the family finances, we were able to bury her using the Penny Policy she had taken out many years before. It also paid for the funeral expenses and the outstanding grocery bill we accrued whilst struggling to emulate her housekeeping skills during her short hospital stay and in the time before she died.

My mother had been the beating heart of our family, and I was devastated at losing her while I was still a teenager living at home. It created a big hole in my life, and I grieved for many years after her death; there was an emptiness inside me that took a long time to heal.


Despite this loss, I realised that life had to go on, and after a few months at work I managed to be promoted to the city drawing office in Norwich. My new local government job was a secure and reputable position, and I was proud to earn the £120 a year salary. I needed to travel over fifty miles a day there and back in all weathers on my old BSA Bantam motorbike and had to undertake the long ride to work even when I was not feeling up to it.

That winter was so cold that I could hardly pull the brake and clutch levers, and my chest felt like a block of ice, although on my father's recommendation I was covered with newspapers for bodily warmth. I had to conserve petrol, which cost three shillings a gallon back then, so I was rarely able to feel the thrust of my bike as I opened the freezing throttle. Except for on one occasion when I lay on the tank, legs up and head down behind the small fairing, streamlining myself as the speedometer hit eighty miles per hour. I was disappointed to discover later that speedos were about 10 per cent fast, so I had barely been doing seventy!

Each morning when I arrived on the outskirts of Norwich city, I rode into a field, changed into my pinstriped three-piece dark suit, rolled up my pitiful riding gear, strapped it onto the pillion and continued on to the office.

I felt rather important and greatly enjoyed my work. I was given a large wooden easel and enough art equipment to create what was wanted, and my desk had a formal label: 'Graham Whiting Junior Graphic Trainee Artist'. I don't think my colleagues in the office ever knew what I had to cope with every day in order to get to work, in respect of travelling for miles in the bitter wintry weather. All they saw each morning was a rather dapper suited young man with gleaming shoes and a black umbrella walking down Castle Street, looking rather like the man about town.

By that time, in contrast to the agreeable hours I spent at work, home was not such a happy place. After our mother died, my best friend and younger sister, Dawn, went away to live with our older sister, Kim, in her luxurious home in Sussex, and I felt abandoned. It seemed to happen suddenly, apparently without any warning – one day Kim arrived in her stylish MG sports car and whisked Dawn off for a new life in East Grinstead. For a few days I didn't realise what had happened, and I think my father was somewhat bemused too.

Travelling fifty miles each day on a small two-stroke motorcycle to and from my place of work, I felt like a real man of the world, though rather an unhappy one. Returning home after work and finding Dawn's empty room left me feeling sad and lonely; a loneliness that had been growing since all my other siblings had one by one left home. And it didn't help that we had a lodger who smoked and drank to excess and was rarely out of bed when I got back after my day at the office.

One winter's evening after a long period at work, drawing and colouring the Kings Lynn town map, a huge assignment for one so young, I left

Norwich after having changed back into my rough travel clothes in the corner of the field.

The way from Norwich to Acle was winding, and I hardly opened the throttle; not because the snow-covered road was dangerous, but because I scarcely had any petrol left. I remember looking into the tank before starting out and seeing only a dribble, so I knew I might make it to Acle, though I would certainly run out after then.

As I left Acle and headed towards the straight eight-mile road to Yarmouth, the bike gurgled to a halt. No one stopped or took any notice, so I started pushing my motorbike along the desolate and frozen road. It was snowing, it was dark, I was cold and I didn't reach Yarmouth until ten o'clock that night, exhausted and frozen to the bone.

What would I do tomorrow when I needed to get to the office? That was for another day, but that night I had to eat sage and onion stuffing as there was nothing else in the cupboard and nothing with which to make sandwiches for the next day. This was a common occurrence at that time as my father wasn't able to earn much and was grieving for my mother; he missed her so much he wasn't able to cope with the responsibility of the household. For a short while, my older brother, Reg, and his wife took me to live with them and their family, and I was very grateful for their kindness in temporarily taking me into their home.

While I was a junior graphic draughtsman, I had met an ex-soldier who took over as manager of the drawing office. Talking with him had given me the idea of seeking 'bed and breakfast' in HM Forces. In May 1962 I finally took up his suggestion to visit the Army Careers Office, and I enlisted.

# CHAPTER 6

# THE ARMY AND MARRIAGE

I joined the army and moved away from the town where my mother's weary body had been laid to rest and away from the job I enjoyed. My work at the council, although pleasant, had felt like it would lead to my being office-bound for the rest of my career with only the thought of a pension and a bent back at the end of my working life. This is what the other draughtsmen seemed to be preoccupied in talking about and even looking forward to, and I knew it wasn't the path for me. Within four weeks I was on the train to London with instructions to find my way to Inkerman Barracks in Woking for basic training in the Corps of Royal Military Police.

Her Majesty gave me ten shillings and a rail warrant for the trip to enlist, but my lack of worldliness made the task of getting from Liverpool Street station to Waterloo with one change at Bank, an absolute nightmare. I had never even heard of the London Underground and had no idea that a train could go underground without puffing steam! Yet, on I went into what seems to me now to have been another dark abyss; and there was no going back.

I arrived four hours late for my appointment at the guardroom, so was reprimanded in the very first minute of my army life as I stepped through the guardroom door to the shout of:

'Where the f***ing hell have you come from, soldier – Timbuk-f***ing-too?'

What a greeting! I stood bolt upright as the duty sergeant stepped towards me from behind the guardroom desk and gnashed his perfect teeth, his breath emanating tobacco. He moved ever closer until our noses touched and my face was covered in spit. I could see my reflection in his eyeballs, but couldn't budge because one of his boots was trapping my foot on the guardroom floor. So this is the army, I thought. This is the kind of greeting a young lad of seventeen receives after taking the Queen's shilling, ready to fight for his country!

All the new recruits wore drainpipe trousers with fourteen-inch bottoms and a long draped jacket as was the fashion in 1962, our top pocket adorned with a spiked pretend handkerchief. Blue suede beetle crushers were the preferred footwear of most young men when rock and roll ruled and Teddy Boys walked the streets looking for trouble and a window in which to admire their hair. So this is how we arrived for basic training. How the guardroom sergeant laughed as he stripped me and took my clothes away, replacing them with baggy khaki-coloured army denims. I never saw my clothes again, and when I look back I wonder how I ever thought they were appealing. Though later on, after years of army uniform, I learned to crave wearing mufti again.

Inkerman Barracks was an old prison built by Spanish prisoners captured from the Peninsular War. It was a stark, frightening and uncomfortable place for a young lad who was putting on a uniform for the first time. Its dark walls and eerie, reputedly haunted bell tower mortuary, which I had to visit during my night patrols on guard duty, made me miss home and I felt very alone, effectively spinning in a random orbit without a centre.

I'd lost my dear mother just a year before enlistment, and on my first night in the army I lay in bed sobbing, lonely and unable to come to terms with the path I'd chosen. But there I was, since the recruiting officer had insisted that this was the toughest corps in which to enlist in order to become a man. I was not the only young soldier sobbing. I could hear others trying to hide their sorrows under the wire-like army blankets covering their young bodies.

Would I become a man? Would I miss the sage and onion stuffing? Would I hell! I was on a mission, a mission to manhood, and I was not going backwards!

As I lay in bed on that first night, I asked myself: why did I enlist? What was the principal reason? Would it prove to be a wise choice? In those dark barracks I heard many alarming and discouraging stories from days gone by; the scary barber and his wicked cuts; terrible events in the drill square where I died a thousand deaths; ghastly incidents in the wooden Nissan huts where we lived, and which were called 'spiders' because from above they looked like giant tarantulas.

On my second day in the army all new arrivals were marched to the quartermaster's store to be kitted out. Battle dress uniform, hairy, itchy and damp army shirts, underpants that could fit over a London bus, brassed webbing and boots as hard as steel. These were my first issued army uniforms.

The boots were called ammunition boots and were clad with one hundred studs, perfectly geometrically spaced so that the sound of gunfire rose up from our feet as we marched. The quartermaster bid one of his assistants measure my chest, and when I saw the tape reading I inhaled every bit of air I could, to try and make myself bigger than I was – but it only registered thirty-two inches. His response to my dimensions was that the army didn't make clothes to fit shrimps.

'Get a body, man!' yelled my squad corporal.

I was in basic training in 1962, the year of the great freeze. I was aware that there was a problem with Cuba, and the Cuban Missile Crisis finally erupted in October of that year. But at that time, given my young age, I was somewhat oblivious to the world picture. It was a time when the United Kingdom could so easily have been sucked into a nuclear war. It was also the start of the Vietnam War and the Cold War struggled on. What a time to choose to become a trained soldier.

Life at the barracks was as tough as it could possibly be. Having a good education with A-levels meant that I was quickly moved towards Sandhurst for officer training, as my Uncle Glyn, a full colonel in the Coldstream Guards, had claimed me for his regiment. He thought it wasn't done for an educated Whiting to be in the ranks of the Royal Military Police (RMP), and that I needed the infantry. Although he shouldn't have admitted it to me, he told me he loathed the Military Police.

All of my uncles had been in WWI as well as WWII. Uncle Glyn and his brother, Fred, were both colonels who were wounded in WWII and had many stories to tell. My maternal uncle, Jim, was a Cockleshell Hero – one of the ten Royal Marines who, in 1942, canoed almost a hundred miles behind enemy lines in a secret and daring WWII mission to blow up the German ships moored at Bordeaux.

I later passed my Regular Commissions Board for entry to officer training. But by the time the results reached me I'd settled so well into the RMP, was excelling as an athlete and gymnast and had made such strong friendships, that I turned down the chance of a commission and continued in the ranks, much to the chagrin of my uncle.

I was told by a wise officer, and also by my father, that the ultimate was to be an officer who had served in the ranks, as that was the only way of understanding the life of an ordinary soldier. He was right, and when I was eventually commissioned I never failed to honour the soldiers I commanded. I always showed them great respect which was returned threefold.

Our training was especially tough, because military policemen had to be fully trained infantry soldiers before taking on a military police role. After some brainwashing by the NCOs (non-commissioned officers), I believed that this was the finest way to be a soldier.

Punishments during basic training were often barbaric, and physical abuse was handed out by the non-commissioned officers who were our gods, as they could make us do whatever they wished. Many were sadistic, and they were very capable of picking on a nine stone weakling with a public school accent who could read and write and who chose to study literature and poetry whilst in training. Perfect credentials for being picked on?

In those days, minor criminals were often given the choice of going down or joining the army. Young offenders mixed with college boys, builders, plumbers, unemployed chaps from poor backgrounds and a few army-mad sons of fathers with military experience. Conscription had ended a few years before I joined, and now the army seemed to be a place of remediation for young men who had lost their way in life, many of whom were quite frightening.

There were the Durham miners, the thieves from Liverpool and the tough, hard criminals from London who we called 'the razor boys' – all of whom the army was charged with transforming. Many were changed and did very well, and I certainly made friends with a few. But some had real mental health issues or displayed violent behaviour and told sick tales of their sexual exploits; most probably lies based on wishful thinking and all foreign to me as I'd led such a sheltered life.

My nickname at school had been 'Skinny Whiting' for a good reason, but in early army training I was referred to as 'Posh Eddie' because I was seen as posh, even though I actually wasn't. Later on, my seniors called me 'Filberticus' because I was into classics and ancient history. At some point I gained the epithet of 'Tiger' which stuck with me throughout my army service and for many years after I left. I didn't mind being teased and the teasing was always good-humoured, so it did give me a sense of belonging.

There was, however, a particularly cruel sergeant who used to call me some terrible names. One day on parade, he asked me if I had a mother. I replied that I did not as she had recently died. He pushed his drill stick into my chest and moved his ugly face closer to mine, gnashing his teeth like the guardroom sergeant had done on my first day. His bright red and black plastic peaked cap was touching my nose, and he proceeded to taunt me, spitting in my face as he bellowed:

'Have you got a mummy, soldier?'

I stood stock still and shouted back as loud as I could,

'Yes, sergeant!'

He then made some particularly offensive remarks about my mother. Deeply insulted and feeling horribly maligned, I bit my tongue and stood still to attention while I wrestled with the snake of wrath in my stomach, almost lashing out with my fists.

At that moment I craved a reversal of roles – and this came to pass some years later, when I was commissioned and commandant of a TAVR (Territorial Army Voluntary Reserve) Centre. At an officer's mess ball one evening, just as the first course was finished and the plates were being taken away, I noticed a smart well-manicured hand reach across the table to serve me. It was him, the sergeant who had mistreated me during training and said such insulting things about my mother. He didn't recognise me, so after supper when the officers withdrew for brandy, I went to the kitchen, looked him in the eye and asked him if he remembered me. He stared right through me as if I wasn't there, but I could sense his discomfort and see the guilt and regret written all over his face. He knew who I was – I didn't need to remind him or say anything; my steady gaze and higher rank were enough to put him in his place.

I passed all the examinations in drill, map reading, weapon training, physical training, battle tests, combat survival, military law and police work and was able to gain high overall marks for my basic training.

Despite the many challenges, my early army career was actually most interesting, and my father said it made me a man. Straight after passing out as a fully trained infantry soldier and military police officer in October 1962, I was given a brief, though highly regarded posting to The Supreme Headquarters of the Allied Powers (SHAPE) in Europe, at Fontainebleau near Paris. There I glimpsed the most senior service officers of the world – generals, admirals, air vice Marshalls and other distinguished war chiefs.

I even 'met' President John F. Kennedy, Eisenhower (Ike) and Charles de Gaulle; well actually, I glanced at them from the corner of my eye whilst standing to attention on security duty with my eyes fixed on the horizon! Ike gave me a nod and a wink from his all-knowing face as he passed along the ranks, inspecting us all.

Back in the UK in November 1962, there was talk of a cold winter to come, so we all waited excitedly for the snow to fall whilst we occupied our freezing billets. Our only source of warmth was a tall ancient cast-iron nineteenth century boiler into which we shoved anything that would burn. By the time the snow eventually came, I was a fully trained soldier. In the icy conditions, I was given a shovel and other crude implements to sweep away the snow. I almost froze to death – we all nearly did. My ammunition boots were literally frozen to my feet, and the eight hours a day that I was on snow clearing made me rather resentful of my new life as a fully trained infantry soldier and military police non–commissioned officer. This certainly was not the active service for which I had trained.

To make things even worse, some experienced soldiers arrived in the training camp from the Far East, showing off their bronzed skin and laughing at the newly trained soldiers clearing snow. These hardened military policemen were on a compulsory rest period which the army called re-acclimatisation.

That year it was so cold that many people in Great Britain died. It was during the last week of snow clearing that I took my motorcycle test. I had to learn to control a skid on ice, so the barrack square was used for training as it was like an ice rink.

Many of us skidded off the square, to be shouted at by the regimental sergeant major, commonly known as the regimental scary monster. We quickly got back on our bikes and struggled to stay on, to taunting chants from friends and junior NCOs. I first learned the word 'beasting' at that time because one of the riders, Fred, was so incompetent that he was sworn at and marched to the guardroom for a beasting, and when he was released, his reports of his time in the 'nick' were horrendous. In today's army, people have little idea what kinds of punishments were handed out under the name of army discipline. It was often abusive, humiliating, nonsensical and downright inhuman, but we took it. We had to!

In 1963 I was offered a place to become a motorcycle rider in the Royal Military Police Motorcycle Display Team, and I travelled and performed throughout Great Britain. My trusty training steed was an extremely powerful khaki coloured 1939 BSA 500cc side-valye machine.

For the show performances, I was given an impressive Triumph TRW 500cc side-valve motorcycle. I rode in front of The Queen on two occasions, at The Edinburgh Tattoo and The Royal Tournament. In 1964 I was in Northern Ireland with my bike, which had been craned onto the passenger ferry at Heysham for transport across the Irish Sea. When we landed in Ireland I was brimming with enthusiasm and excitement, and after a few hours we had assembled our machines and hit the road towards Lisburn Garrison, our home during the display season.

During the Northern Ireland Show, the winning rider earned a date with Miss Northern Ireland. This 'queen of the show' had not previously revealed herself – she was described as the new Northern Ireland Greta Garbo. I tried so hard to win, and when I was eventually declared the best rider of the day, I got to go on the blind date; and what a blind date it was! I was told to meet Maraid outside the local Lisburn cinema, and at first I didn't recognise her from the description I'd been given. All I was told by my sergeant major was that I couldn't miss her beauty, her flowing dress, her stunning hourglass figure and her splendid hairdo. I looked around and finally out of the early evening sun came this vision.

She was as embarrassed as I was. As I stuttered and plucked up courage to look into her beautiful green Irish eyes, I gulped and realised from the look on her face that I was not the handsome dude she'd expected. I was so pleased the date was short. After we'd finished the prepared meal, we strolled along the local riverbank and talked of life, horses and motorcycles. I said goodnight and walked her to her home like a real soldier and gentleman. To my amazement, the following evening I received a proposal of marriage.

What the hell was going on? It seemed real, and rising from the envelope was a perfume that I can still smell today. After opening it and finding an even stronger rose-smelling letter, sprinkled with pressed rose petals, I heard a giggle from the corner of our billet. The rotters! I was downcast – who needs friends like that?!

As a young soldier, it was deemed prudent to have a wife before one went overseas on active service, and in 1964 I met Rosemary, a lovely young woman born in Ireland and whose family then lived in Nayland, Suffolk, where the villagers held her in high esteem.

Rosemary loved to dance and we were a regular dance couple in local dance halls, often winning prizes for our jive. She had qualified as a psychiatric nurse the year before we met and was adored by her patients in the large Essex mental hospital where she worked. I used to ignore the rules and visit her in her room when she was having a break from her shift, although such visits were not allowed. One evening I was seen by the matron and legged it in full uniform, struggling to find a way out. In my attempts to escape I inadvertently passed many rooms where psychiatric night treatments were being carried out – activities which Rosemary had warned me about. Some of these involved ECT (electroconvulsive therapy) and plunging patients into boiling and freezing baths, all of which looked and sounded utterly terrifying. After that experience I never visited her in the hospital again!

In January 1965 Rosemary showed me a scar on her neck, attributed to the biopsy of a lymph gland, which she and her family told me was nothing to worry about. It was not until April 1965, when I was on my PTI course, that I noticed that she was no longer able to dance as easily as she did the year before. And when she became pregnant, we stopped dancing and focused on preparing for our future together. I had no idea then, that her family knew she had a potentially terminal illness and were keeping it secret from both me and Rosemary.

I had a good relationship with Rosemary's family, particularly her warmhearted mother, and they were always very generous, showering me with gifts, including a car. However, there was a great deal of secrecy, and the most crucial facts were kept hidden. When Rosemary and I decided to get married they didn't tell either of us that she was seriously ill with Hodgkin's lymphoma. Keeping a terminal diagnosis from a patient, especially one so young, was not unknown back in those days – but they also made the judgment not to tell me. So with both of us unaware of the ominous prognosis hanging over us, we were married in May 1965 in a Catholic ceremony at the Church of the Sacred Heart in Nayland. It was attended by the extended family, friends from school and some soldiers who I was serving with at the time. My great schoolfriend, Colin Burns, was my best man.

After our wedding, we moved into an army rental at Roussillon Barracks in Chichester. Rosemary came from quite a well-off family and wasn't happy in the army accommodation, which was only of a very basic standard. So I was allowed to find somewhere outside the barracks, and during the rest of my time in the army we lived in various rented houses in Selsey, West Wittering and Old Bosham. The last house was our favourite – a high-class home owned by a London barrister who gave it to us for a low rent.

During that year, as well as continuing to serve in the army, I studied medical science. I was released for four evenings a week and travelled on my motorcycle to London University (UCL) for a night school course. I was able to leave the barracks well ahead of time for the journey from Chichester to UCL as my work schedule often finished at lunchtime. My professor, Andrew Huxley, and his team of lecturers were open to me being the only soldier with aspirations to study medicine when I eventually finished my service. This was a really stimulating and exciting time for me, and at the age of twenty I was learning so much about the foundations of medicine.

When it was suggested by one of the lecturers that I consider leaving the army and coming to UCL full time, I knew I wouldn't be able to leave the forces until my time was up and I would have to wait. I had also applied to read medicine at Oxford and PPE at Warwick and could have been released early from the army to take up a university place. But I knew that Rosemary wasn't well and needed my help; which meant that I couldn't possibly focus on a degree of any magnitude. So I opted out, deferred my place and stayed on in the army.

I had to get on with my job, continue to study as hard as I could and prepare for medicine when I left the army. I attended Chichester College of Further Education in 1966 where I sat three science A-levels and repeated O-level English Language and Anatomy and Physiology, taking the London University Board exams to ensure a place at UCL when the time came.

I became a first-time father in 1966 when I was twenty-one. It was a miracle that our daughter, Maxine, was delivered safely and that Rosemary was able to experience unreserved joy in giving birth. Rosemary was a devout Catholic and attended church every week, which gave her much comfort. Although I remained a non-Catholic, I supported Rosemary in her faith, and Maxine was baptised in the Catholic Church. Maxine was a gorgeous baby, and it was incumbent upon me to look after her for the first years of her life due to her mother's illness. I enjoyed the roles of soldier, husband, carer and father during that time, and it seemed natural to multitask in this way.

Rosemary continued to suffer from her cancer throughout my army years, and whenever I was sent away on active service, she would return to live with her mother as she didn't want to be alone. Rosemary's mother was always pleased to have her and Maxine at home with her, and Rosemary had other family in the area with some cousins close by. Rosemary was popular with the other army wives, and they were a kind support to her; though of course, they were unaware of the seriousness of her diagnosis, as she and I were kept in the dark about it.

On leaving the motorcycle display team in 1964, the year I met Rosemary, I had been recommended by my commanding officer to become a physical training instructor (PTI), and I won a place at The Army School of Physical Training in Aldershot. My first preparatory course was at the Army School of Physical Training (ASPT) in Shorncliffe, Kent, to be 'beasted' again and made physically ready to enter that illustrious mecca of fitness and manliness.

The ASPT at Shorncliffe was a really tough training camp with an eight-week course, followed by two six-month courses, back-to-back; a hell of a place to learn the greatest job in the army. Coincidentally my father had completed the same course when he was in uniform in 1921.

Reveille was at 6 a.m. and each day was extremely physically demanding, with contact time beginning at 6 a.m. and ending at 9 p.m., six days a week. I assessed my contact time for those courses and compared it with my son's contact time at university last year. In those three courses, I had five times as much contact time with my teachers and trainers in that one year as he did during the whole of his three-year degree course.

Each day of training, the morning started with a four-mile run, carrying packs laden with five house bricks. And twice a week the run was extended to ten miles with four house bricks. The straps of the rucksack cut into my shoulders and created such pain that it was hard to bear, especially when the pack bumped up and down and the weight of the bricks came banging down on my shoulders. There was no such thing as trainers in those days, only a thin pair of the army's infamous khaki plimsolls. When our feet were sore and ripped up with blisters, they sometimes bled into our boots, and then Brufen was prescribed, for no soldier dared complain about anything, least of all pain. To a suggestion of any discomfort, my sergeant major retorted,

'Whiting, pain is only a sensation, just like having sex!'

Being fit and very competitive, I was taking steps towards what the army offered young people like me: a life of physical activity, hard challenges and the opportunity to learn harsh discipline. So I grinned and put up with it all.

I graduated with First Class Honours from the Army Physical Training School, having passed the required physical disciplines in respect of performance, theory of teaching physical training, and coaching in a number of disciplines. I was awarded a Diploma in Physical Education, a coveted credential for a training that was far more intensive than a modern degree. It was essentially a top-class extensive in-depth teaching qualification. The last diploma of this kind was issued in 1972, and today the content of that course would qualify for a much higher award.

The ASPT offered excellent facilities for physical education, having around a dozen rugby pitches shared with the local community, and several gymnasia, especially the famous Fox and Wand Tetley gyms where outstanding physical training teachers in many areas of physical education were created by the talented staff. A couple went on to become renowned gymnastics coaches, and a few even became Olympians.

The army school had a superb swimming pool with high boards, so I could dive whenever I wished. I was never a champion swimmer, since I was too heavy. Even so, I developed an array of high dives and competed successfully in the Inter-Services Championships. I won some acclaim, especially for high-board diving, and once performed the feat of a handstand double from a 10-metre board.

One day during training, my fellow trainees and I were mustered at the pool and presented with a challenge I will never forget. Two hairy army swimmers, both APTC physical training instructors, were high up on a platform above the pool, holding a trapeze, grinning maliciously and posing outrageously with huge bulging arm and leg muscles.

We were all commanded to perform long swing-to-reverse multiple somersaults off the trapeze into the water before being allowed to lunch. I think I spun over seven, into water broken by jets from a hosepipe. It was a terrifying stunt, and the speed of the rotation was really frightening. Many young trainees who were not divers, refused to perform and were denied lunch. They were encouraged to report that evening for extra diving lessons and a chat with the instructors. They were told that they had two choices. One was to resist and leave the army, the other was to do what was required off the trapeze. They all did the latter; what a way to overcome fear and achieve on a high level!

On another occasion, we were marched to Fox gymnasium where we all gathered around a boxing ring. This was the dreaded test of courage called 'milling' which consisted of wearing sixteen-ounce boxing gloves while each soldier was paired off with a soldier of a similar weight and thrust into the ring. We all had to show three minutes of courage, with increasing exhaustion and blood and snot pouring from our often broken noses, as we hammered one another for what seemed like hours until the bell sounded. You earned a reputation as either a great and brave chap or a coward.

I was at that time boxing as a light-heavyweight. All potential physical training instructors had to box as part of their training and qualification. They needed to qualify not only as able boxers, but also as boxing coaches and referees after they had experienced the milling. Imagine that in today's world of Health and Safety!

By the time I finished my third qualification as a sports coach and after two years of daily gym workouts and weight training, I qualified to box at heavyweight level. Having joined the army as a lightweight, by the time I was actively teaching physical education I weighed sixteen stones, so a boxing bout was a relatively simple affair. The punches didn't really hurt much, except for one fight against a lance sergeant in the Coldstream Guards who was six feet nine and weighed nineteen stones. He beat me easily, so I spent months training in the gym, pumping iron, skipping, bench-pressing, squatting and attempting all the other training schedules I could find, until I felt like a wound-up spring.

After all that intensive training I was in great physical shape, ready to challenge anyone at anything and pretty sure I could handle any test the army might throw at me, especially the rematch the following year. It began well with me leading the fight and feeling confident about my prospects of a win – until halfway through round three when, with relative complacency, I walked straight into a right hook, breaking my jaw and losing the fight – a painful experience on various levels!

In my new life as a fighting fit PTI, I sometimes looked back and remembered the terrible feeling of being picked on when I was a skinny teenager in Yarmouth. I imagined that I might seek out the ruffians from my schooldays in order to avenge myself or obtain some sort of justice. I never did, though, and I don't think many people do; except that occasionally one might inadvertently bump into former assailants and see them with fresh eyes for who they really are.

Outside of working hours and in holiday times, in addition to all my formal training, I used to go to circuses and funfairs and enter arm wrestling and boxing competitions. It was good fun, helped improve fitness and you could earn £5 for a win. When I wasn't engaged in these pursuits, I often visited my sister, Dawn, and on a couple of occasions was able to help her out by stepping in and having words with her boyfriend at the time.

After my mother died my father spent nearly twenty years living on his own in our Yarmouth house. It was hard for him to remain there with all his memories, and he was lonely as most of the family had moved away. His children were spread far and wide, living in Australia, New Zealand, Germany, Canada and many parts of England. So visiting him regularly was difficult for some of us, but we did our best and kept in close touch with him through letters and phone calls. I generally called my father every week, and he called me too and sent me beautifully written letters.

In my spare time I also continued my passion for fishing, mainly carp angling. I was a member of The British Carp Study Group (BCSG), whose protocols were at the pinnacle of serious carp fishing. It was about honouring the fish you would or wouldn't catch, taking care of the water and making sure that you were fishing with respect for the whole carp lake. I loved talking with other anglers about the science of carp fishing, the intelligence, the beauty, the serenity and the utter magnificence of the carp, and I imbibed an intense love for the world of water. As a result of which, I've written many articles on fishing over the years for various fishing magazines. When I caught a large carp, a little under 30 lbs, in the 1960s, it seemed as if I would never need to catch another; although I later went on to success in both carp angling and salmon fly fishing.


From the mid-1960s I was engaged in some remarkable activities, sanctioned and paid for by the army. The army afforded me many opportunities to experience challenging situations, and I don't mind admitting that I often had to struggle hard to overcome some of the more difficult ones.

During the Greek and Turkish hostilities I was posted to Cyprus for six months as part of the United Nations peacekeeping force. Various off-duty activities were organised to keep the troops entertained, and in Cyprus I did my most notable long distance swim. It was a distance of 20 miles from Akrotiri to Episkopi, in a sea as flat as a mill pond, and the winner was awarded a trip home on full pay. Although I didn't win, my colonel sent me home for a week anyway, as he said I deserved it since I was so heavy that I didn't easily float! I fell in love with the country, but on my tour of duty I discovered first-hand the painful and horrific nature of war. I had terrifying experiences and found myself in intensely difficult situations in which good friends of mine were killed. I can clearly recall the incidents, but a soldier tends not to want to look back or to speak about these things.

After Cyprus I was posted to Borneo, and one day I found myself in a section of ten soldiers, cutting our way through dense jungle with machetes. Carrying a sharpening stone was mandatory, as the bamboo and other undergrowth blunted our machetes in hours, so we often needed to sharpen them.

On this particular day we were led by a local scout whose task was to keep an eye on where we were going. Having walked a few hundred metres through a leech-infested swamp, we climbed onto a bank and began to de-leech ourselves, with blood oozing out and trickling down our legs, as we pulled the creatures off.

We then went on our way, keeping to the narrow paths and hacking through the jungle. A few hundred metres on, we came to another clearing where I saw a small tree a few metres in front of me, about six feet tall and swaying gently in the wind; or so I thought.

Mai, our scout, pulled me back from walking towards the tree. With his finger on his lips and suddenly rooted to the spot, he whispered to stand still, not to move and to watch him for signals. My eyes were transfixed on the small sapling which began to sway from side to side a little. I was waiting for instructions.

'Cobra, king cobra!'

I withdrew slightly, as I could now see that my 'tree' was a big brown creamy-hooded venomous snake, easily fifteen feet long and extremely dangerous. It was hissing like a steam kettle and clearly angry at our presence. My dripping wet body stiffened with fear. Snakes are lacking in focused eyesight and are deaf but can sense vibrations, so I locked my muscles to ensure there was no movement. Mai told me that such a snake can cause death within an hour and can strike accurately from over eight feet. We were about ten feet away and ready to flee.

'Don't run,' whispered Mai.

I could see a hole near the snake, next to which a number of new-born baby cobras, actually sweet but potentially menacing, were sunning themselves in the warm flickering jungle sunlight. I had been briefed that a new-born cobra can hunt with venom from the minute it is born.

Our section stood still and watched, though one man who was terrified, clutched his submachine gun and cocked the bolt in readiness to blow this great snake to bits. I put my hand on his weapon and glared at him, which didn't make him at all happy.

After a while the cobra, with head slowly dropping and waving from side to side, fell to the ground and withdrew into the hole followed by its carpet of young. I tried to count the number of babies that accompanied their mother down into the den but stopped at eight.

That was the end of this unusual confrontation, so I thanked Mai and we headed back to camp to live another day. We had a story to tell!

My adventures were not confined to overseas deployments. My brother, John, when he was at Loughborough College of Physical Education in 1952, shared accommodation with Peter Gordon Lawrence who made the first fibreglass moulded canoe, and the first two of these new craft graced the sitting room where they both lived.

John supported Peter in his endeavours, effectively pioneering the move from wood and canvas canoes to glass fibre. In 1956, when I was only twelve, he had organised a canoeing trip to Denmark. John arrived at our house in Great Yarmouth with six of his students, having bought a well-used 1942 single-decker bus. As they arrived, I saw the roof was covered in canoes, and it was then that I decided that one day I would follow my brother's lead.

Only ten years later when I was an army PTI, I was involved in planning and leading some remarkable canoeing adventures. The first was to paddle canoes from Carlisle to Colchester with a team of six and over one hundred portages. This was a massive undertaking and was co-led by one of my sergeants. It was the trip of a lifetime, which was then followed by an even more challenging expedition which involved a canoeing trip from Padstow around Land's End to Bournemouth. The team of eight soldiers were very keen and we were equipped with WWII canvas canoes with enough space to store all the equipment we needed.

Anyone who has taken on such a journey will know the tidal hazards, the often rough and less often calm waters that are a feature of these sea trips and the variable weather one encounters. I was fortunate to experience this trip over two weeks, camping on beaches and living on army rations. I had an intrepid team and during our expedition we climbed coastal rock faces and invented a new activity which I called 'rock jumping'.

This involved finding steep vertical rock faces, climbing to quite high natural rock platforms and leaping off into the sea. I was careful to first investigate the water with my snorkel and mask to gauge the depth and safety for these jumps. We never had an accident, but I remember a number of unmentionable expletives during our jumps.

As we reached Salcombe, we were exhausted. We'd used up almost all of our repair kits, and as well as being very tired, one or two of the team had diarrhoea. The mackerel and pollack, caught on seagull feathers and littering the bottoms of our canoes, were a reminder that some of the fish we'd baked over beach fires had probably been undercooked.

Just east of Starthole Bay, as the river meets the sea, we paddled eastwards past the notorious Wolf Rock at the entrance to Salcombe harbour, and I christened six huge jumps about a mile from the harbour's mouth. It was essential to have a crew in canoes next to where I would jump so that if anything went wrong I could be rescued. Every one of the soldiers jumped from 'Heaven', the highest rock at about sixty-five feet, and it became one of my regiment's main summer activities. I took soldiers there from Chichester at least a dozen times from 1966 to 1969, with three of those trips launched in mid-winter.

Looking ahead a quarter of a century, and every upper school student in my school would engage in performing those same rock jumps near Salcombe. In the 1980s our pioneering coastal adventures of sea swimming, diving, rock climbing and rock jumping were given the new combined name of 'coasteering'. Coasteering expeditions are now offered by many activity centres, with some including the study of coastal ecology.

In 1967, after passing all three phases for my physical training diploma, I was recommended to work towards joining the Army Physical Training Corps (APTC). I was at that time a corporal at the Royal Military Police Training Depot in Chichester.

Roussillon Barracks in Chichester, where I was based, was one of the army's newest training depots and had everything a young PTI needed: a large gymnasium, boxing rings and access to lots of outdoor space. It was a fully equipped military establishment, and the only element that I didn't enjoy was the number of young recruits who were persecuted by wand-wielding NCOs strutting around the camp as if they were the bee's knees. Very few of them were kind to recruits, though as I was then an NCO PTI and worked in the world of fitness and muscle, I was pretty much a law unto myself. Everyone looked up to the PTIs, even the other power-mad NCOs. My task was very rewarding and interesting as it involved daily contact with the recruits in training and the permanent staff, with some exciting things to do.

My three years of both delivering and receiving extensive training was particularly demanding, especially as I was taught and encouraged to constantly push beyond my limits, by some of the country's top martial art professionals; tough, strong, intelligent and highly ranked experts like Tom Shaw.

Army life in general was very testing, and with the strictures and structures needed to weld the many different characters into a cohesive operational unit, it was difficult to just be yourself. There were the usual underlying tensions and conflicts between people living and working at such close quarters, but I was protected from physical confrontations because I was the senior PTI in martial arts disciplines connected to Ju-jitsu and Aikido, along with traditional military unarmed combat and self-defence. I suffer now from osteoarthritis as a result of my extensive martial arts training. Would I have opted out if I had known when embarking on this part of my army life that such a painful condition would strike when I was older? No!

As a PTI, I taught many soldiers from the Royal Military Police and also from the infantry and Royal Marines. The courses I ran were to do with self-defence and unarmed combat – the kinds of skills in which a soldier might need to be proficient during active service. At that time, Afghanistan and Iraq were not on my page, but the Far East was part of my brief. I offered these courses for more than three years and met many fine men amongst those I taught – plus of course, the usual few cocky fools who were just asking to be taken down a peg or two by a well-trained instructor!

# CHAPTER 7

# ARMY BOSSES

A longside the many positives, there was a notable fly in the ointment of my life as a PTI.

My boss in the PT department was a short, mean, muscle-bound member of the Army Physical Training Corps (APTC). He was to be my 'controller' for three years from when I was appointed PTI in 1965, until 1968.

Boxing, wrestling, tactical advances to battle (TABs), regular morning forced marches, runs and self-defence based on Aikido and Ju-jitsu were the order of the day. The latter was my particular speciality and in my role it behoved me to make the rest of the soldiers on the course look up to me and believe that I was the toughest soldier on camp, exceptionally experienced and always ready for combat and training.

However, this APTC boss tried to belittle the PT staff daily, and he always knew best. He sported the cross-swords on his white woolly jumper for all to see that he was king of the PT staff. He was morose, controlling and smoked a pipe, just like the colonel. He was never on time in the mornings and the four PTIs essentially ran the depot's fitness and battle tactics programme.

Our boss, 'the little man', was a hammer thrower and each morning he and I would meet on the depot athletics field, with me trotting obediently behind him across the drill-square, lugging all our weapons of practice. He carried his 16 lb hammer, while I struggled with a huge khaki army issued barrow which held my high jump stands, javelins, discuses, three more 16 lb shots and other necessary measuring devices. We did a few laps of the 400 metre track together, him smoking his pipe and me, long-legged, a foot taller and inwardly grinning at his every step. He didn't fully understand my scorn, and perhaps he wasn't bright enough to pick it up, but our interactions only served to increase my antipathy.

I don't like to use the word 'hate', but it's hard to find another to express my feeling. Despite my efforts to the contrary, I found myself despising my boss, as he was just such an unbelievably poor leader. How he got into the APTC, I will never know. At no time did I ever see him teach; the nearest was when he wanted to coach me on the high bar. He would laugh to try and humiliate me when I fell and then rapidly switch to anger and aggression to try and intimidate me into doing better – not the most helpful approach!

I did fall quite often and over the course of a couple of years suffered many injuries through trying to do what he was expecting. One day he suggested I throw a new dismount to make my routine more exciting. On the gym floor there was only a one-inch thick coconut mat, measuring eight feet by six. He wanted me to do a reverse double back somersault dismount, rarely performed in those days though still used today in Olympic gymnastics. At a weight of about 100 kilos, I had to get it right.

I managed, in the course of a couple of hours, to throw six good dismounts. By then I was naturally quite confident, and when the colonel inspected, my boss wanted to show off his PT staff, so I was called forward to do a double in front of him. Unfortunately, that one time, I got it completely wrong. Having over-rotated, I landed on my backside and broke three coccygeal vertebrae. I was unable to perform the trick again, and my bones took a year to heal properly, restricting my range of activities for a while. Such was the power of the coach and his desire to show the colonel what a great chap he was.

I was an able competitor in most field events, and when I threw the hammer twenty-four feet further than my boss's best, he confined me to the other field events so he could still be the 'hammer king'. I was fine with this as I depended on my relationship with this chap for any future promotion, most especially entry to the APTC. He held my life and future in his hands.

Looking back on those days, I can see that one of the most difficult things for me was that my boss just wouldn't allow any avenue of expression for an active and inventive mind. I often suggested new ideas, but it was almost impossible as a relatively junior rank to get him to even consider that I might have a good proposal to help the department. Of course, he knew everything!

For example, I had an aspiration during my PT training courses to perform on the gymnastic high bar to a proficient level. My boss told me I was too big to even consider performing on this equipment and that I should forget it. For weeks, in order to attain success on the bar, I tried to find a way of practising the various essential exercises without being forbidden by his majesty. I was soon to come up with a solution.

One weekend in 1965 after I'd qualified as a PTI, I was in my mother-in-law's garden in Suffolk and noticed a long stainless steel tube, about one and a half inches in diameter and twelve feet long, which for some years had been lying around in the shed next to an old tractor. In the garden were two substantial trees about eight feet apart. I had found the basic elements to create my own garden gym.

From the army equipment store, I borrowed a hemp rope that was thin enough to be pushed right through the entire length of the metal tube. My idea was to appropriate two, one-ton garden rollers (with my mother-in-law's permission!), pass the rope through the hollow bar, and anchor it over two large branches where they grew out of the trunks. I then dug two big holes and secured the long, dangling rope-ends to the roller handles.

All that was needed was to push the rollers into the holes, which enabled the rope to be tightened as much as was necessary to have the bar suspended ready to use, with the rope acting as a tensioner and straightener inside the steel bar. The bar was anchored about eight feet above the ground. It was absolutely safe and hardly moved when I hung on it. I then dug a pit about a metre deep and a metre wide by four metres long to create a system to protect me if I were to perform difficult tricks and fall.

My brother-in-law, Rosemary's brother, was a car fanatic and drove me to a scrapyard where, for £1, I bought six old car seats. I filled the pit I had dug under the bar with the foam from the car seats ripped into small pieces and excitedly did a few dismounts to see if it would protect me when I landed.

After trying some short circles I dismounted in complete safety, so it worked. It was fun, it was great, it was mine and I did it! Throwing a canvas sheet over it, I returned to barracks and waited for my next time off, resisting mentioning anything to my boss. Without sharing the invention with anyone, I took a couple of friends to see the bar.

'Bloody hell, how did you make that?' asked Harry, a much better gymnast than I could ever be. I went through the secret manufacturing process and asked them to keep it secret from the boss.

That afternoon we played around on the bar and it flexed, but it was so stressed by the ropes and rollers which weighed over two tons, that Harry said it was better than the PT school's Olympic high bar. Perhaps it was, yet when I was ready to test the landing area with a trick done by a heavy chap, I was soon to find a flaw – landing in the foam needed some alteration.

Another brother-in-law, my sister Joan's husband who was a meteorologist, acquired a dozen meteorological rubber balloons which were over a metre wide when inflated. Using a dozen of these, inflated to only about 10 per cent of their volume, I threw the floppy rubber balloons on top of the loose foam. It was another eureka moment and I was so happy; I felt I could do any trick and land without injury. Little did I know then that in a few years every car would incorporate a version of my landing balloons: the airbag!

It was a perfect landing area, safe and soft, and for some weeks I played around and took my friends for sessions. They were all impressed, and I was soon ready for it to be revealed. When I attended the next gymnastics course, I was able to throw trick after trick with ease in front of my seething boss.

As well as passing the necessary physical and teaching examinations for entry to the APTC, I had recently passed my officer selection to enter Sandhurst, which my boss really didn't like. He did as much as he could to belittle me and told me that all officers were shit, posh, rich people. Even when I was competing for the local athletics club in the British Nationals, he made sure I was on duty at the same time as my main events were scheduled. Using his rank, he basically undermined me as much as he could.

His belittling was always rather clever, and he would call me into his office and push my buttons. On the day my approval came through to the company office to leave the depot and travel to Sandhurst for my assessment, he cleverly arranged for me to do the morning sixteen-mile TAB, which he scheduled to start at 6 a.m. I was due to be driven to the railway station after that event to take the 1 p.m. train to Aldershot from Chichester, get a connection to Camberley and walk to the Royal Military Academy, Sandhurst. I was ready to get out of the RMP and take a step into an infantry regiment after my commission, which was definitely my first choice, above entering the APTC.

My boss knew that I would be exhausted after the TAB, which would mess up my day; and he had told me behind closed doors in his office, that I was no good to anyone and would never get on. He also told me that he had twice failed to pass officer selection but had anyway declined a commission because he just didn't like officers; he was so obtuse he really thought I believed his story. That day at Sandhurst was possibly the most important in my life at that time.

Despite the boss's attempts at sabotage, later that year my acceptance documents came through from Sandhurst. This was after the army athletics championships and an around Britain tour under the heading of KAPE (Keep the Army in the Public Eye) where we demonstrated unarmed combat throughout a few of the main cities of Britain.

I was summoned to the company office where I sat opposite my CO (commanding officer), a charming, sensitive and eminent, though rather ineffectual man. He told me I could leave the depot and enter officer training at Sandhurst, but first I would need to ask my boss at the gym if I could be spared. My heart sank, and I asked Major West if he could kindly make that decision instead. He responded in the negative and reminded me that there was an army protocol to be followed and that the PT department was vital to the corps.

So I headed off to the gym and gently knocked on the boss's door. He shouted for me to enter and there he sat, smug-faced in his little chair with the furrowed glowering face of officialdom. He asked me why I wanted to disturb him.

'Sir, I have been accepted for officer training at Sandhurst, and I have an interview date. I would be grateful if you would kindly release me from my PT commitments and allow me to attend this final interview, Sir.'

He smirked, frowned, sat back in his chair and puffed harder on his pipe. Apparently the PT department could not do without me – the athletics, the basketball team of which I was captain and the Courses Wing all could not possibly find another NCO to manage the various courses I was engaged in teaching.

'Corporal Whiting, I am against this move. I can't spare you, therefore you need to cancel your application for a commission.'

I was extremely disappointed. As I left his office, I went into the PT staff office where my buddies could clearly see my upset. Turned down by the boss, daily caring for a wife with cancer, raising a baby and being refused the chance to get out of a corps with a boss that I didn't respect, all seemed too much.

The PT staff were aware of my enthusiasm to leave the MPs but knew nothing of my application. When I explained, they protested to the boss on my behalf, and the main man just stood in the gym flexing his muscles, sucking his pipe and told us all that that was the end of the matter.

'Corporal Whiting will be staying at the depot to take the courses as usual until he finishes his service. Besides, he has been recommended for his third stripe from today onwards, so he will be continuing on as a sergeant PTI.'

I had other ideas.

I went home that afternoon to our privately rented house which was called 'Bay's Haven' and was in the lovely upmarket village of Old Bosham near Chichester, yards from Chichester harbour. As usual, when I arrived home I saw my wife and baby daughter waiting at the gate with tea laid ready in our pretty garden. My face said it all. I had been bullied again; rejected and cast down by a five feet one inch tall APTC god.

The next day I was back taking the morning TABs and doing my job teaching Aikido, as the newly promoted PTI Sergeant Whiting; but the promotion meant absolutely nothing.

I was summoned to the CO's office and formally informed of my boss's decision. I accepted it as I was a soldier and all soldiers must do as they are told, must they not? The CO then softened the blow somewhat when he told me that my current APTC boss was imminently to be posted to Hong Kong. With a twinkle in his all-knowing eye and a wink to me, he said that the replacement would be a really terrific boss, and I would get on well with him until I moved on to the APTC. He was an athlete, a boxer and a fitness fanatic.

'Just what you need, sergeant!'

Three weeks later I was ordered to take my old boss to the railway station. And soon after dropping him and his family off, I was to collect my new boss from the same station.

I jumped into the MP Land Rover, enthusiastic to meet the new boss, and drove to Chichester station, full of trepidation. I was sad at not taking a train to Sandhurst, but I had to be open to the future and my destiny.

There he stood outside the station entrance, erect in full military uniform, cross-swords on his tunic jacket and a crown on his forearm signifying his rank. Company Sergeant Major, Royal Army Physical Training Corps, two soft kit bags and a shiny cap badge glimmering in the sun. This looked like a great leader. Maybe life in the RMP would not be that bad after all. Perhaps he would be a better boss; though one thing he had in common with his predecessor was his height at five feet two inches – and I was soon to find out that his ego gave him another six feet!

The short journey to the barracks was an excruciatingly difficult fifteen minutes. My new boss was arrogant, cocky, and a war hero who had accomplished every possible physical skill. He was selected to take the job because he had fully earned such an august posting with the MPs. I only got a few words in, just before we turned into the barracks.

He said he had plans for the depot to be the British Army's main centre for courses in self-defence, and I was to lead these for the rest of my army service. He told me not to worry because the army would put my sick wife in an army hospital somewhere so she could rest in peace, and I could continue in my role and pursue my career. That was the army's way of lessening the effect on me of any future deterioration in my wife's health, yet I knew I couldn't possibly dishonour and destroy my family in this way.

I said nothing until I got home that evening and had sat for a while in an armchair, quietly contemplating my situation. After thinking the whole thing over, I came to the conclusion that it was time to ditch the esteemed much sought-after and hard-earned position as a PTI in the

RMP. I hadn't previously talked in any depth to Rosemary about the extent of my unhappiness with my awful army bosses. Now I had to explain how truly miserable I was and admit that I was ready to leave the army. Fortunately, she understood my plight and was ready to stand by whatever decision I made.

I could see no other way forward than to leave, as my new boss was even worse than the old one. He told me he disliked clever NCOs, that he would be the one who hammered me back into line and that I was to forget Sandhurst.

'Whiting, you can't have a mind of your own. You are the army's mind. I don't like thinkers!'

I appealed, but the CO told me that I had to do as I was told, the army had spent thousands of pounds on training me, I was the senior most qualified unarmed combat and Aikido PTI in the British Army, and that I therefore had to to fulfil my trained-for role and do as I was told.

'Thank you, Sir.'

The next months were such a trial. Not due to nursing a sick wife and caring for a young child, which was a pleasure, but because I felt trapped. I had to get out and get away from what felt like military persecution and control. Although I'd passed the exams and could have joined the APTC in 1969, I had by this time given up any idea of the APTC. If other members of the APTC were like the two bosses who ran the gym at the depot, I wanted nothing to do with that corps.

After finally reaching the decision to leave the army, I asked my colonel for advice about taking a step towards civvy street. He reminded me that I had signed up for twenty-two years and had already turned down a commission early in my service. He told me in no uncertain terms that when a soldier makes a commitment, he must keep it, and if he doesn't he will be a laughing stock. I had an interview with my CO, and he was similarly without any compassion or understanding and did his best to put me off leaving, suggesting I would be foolish to throw away a promising future in the army.

Following the CO's unsympathetic reception, Rosemary and I talked and planned our way out together. At that time we didn't think she would die in the near future as she had given birth without any problems and seemed relatively fit. I was worried about what I might do when I left the army, my main concern being how I would manage to father Maxine and look after Rosemary if I took this big leap into the unknown. Still, I had to do it.

The next day, the colonel made my desire to leave the army known to everyone in the company office, and from that day onwards I was 'sent to Coventry' and given the silent treatment. It soon became clear that wanting to get out of the RMP early was so unusual, no matter what the reasons, that those in charge would feel compelled to take some strong action in order to set an example.

What happened next was a huge blow. I was asked to take up a position in the clothing stores as a quartermaster, issuing uniforms and boots and suchlike. Instead of continuing as a fully-trained, well-experienced and highly regarded PTI, I was to become a storeman!

I refused and began much more rapid steps to leave – I asked my mother-in-law to buy me out. When my intentions were made public, it then became prudent for the CO to have me gone sooner rather than later in case other senior NCOs were tempted to follow me. It was a rapid route to civvy street, and I didn't regret it. Had there been time for a real conversation, and had I been treated as an individual and thanked for the commitment I had made as a serving MP, there might have been some possibility of staying; but it was not to be.

Within a week I was offered the opportunity to end my service with a posting to Hong Kong while my demob was arranged, which might take months. This prized posting was probably offered with a view to encouraging me to stay in the army. It was suggested that whilst I was in Hong Kong, my wife would be put in a convalescent home and my daughter placed in a boarding school. It felt like a heartless way to treat a committed soldier, and I was furious.

It so happened that my Uncle Glyn had served with and knew, the Provost Marshall, who kindly wrote to me and took exception to the walls that were being put up to delay or block my plans to leave. He made it clear that I had been treated with disrespect, given my exceptional commitment to the armed forces. With his help and a quick signature on my discharge form, my discharge was swiftly executed.

I had been committed to my job and succeeded in everything I did, so I received an outstanding recommendation and an exemplary final record from the army before I left. I was also awarded The Cyprus Medal for my active service in 1964 and The Cold War Medal for my years of service during the Cold War.

Three years after I left the army and started teaching, I met the colonel who had signed my discharge papers, at a garden party at Dean Close School in Cheltenham. We exchanged many stories of life in the army, and I kept in touch with him until he passed away some years later. In a twist of fate, I taught his grandson and granddaughter at the school.

In defence of army protocols, I can now see that it is incumbent on leaders to ensure that soldiers become part of a unified force, with their individuality mostly only experienced subliminally or at time of valour. Back in the 1960s I naturally had the views of a young soldier nursing a wife and looking after a child and was not capable of seeing the bigger picture. I can appreciate all the great opportunities the army offered me and have no regrets about my army service. It is only the occasional power-mad soldier with rank who casts a shadow over the otherwise great privilege to serve our country.

My parents, William and Winifred, at their wedding (1921)

Aged 5 with
my younger
sister, Dawn,
aged 2 (1949)

Aged 15 (1959)

My mother, shortly before she died when I was 17 (1961)

Royal Military Police (RMP) - back row, middle (1962)

Holding the hammer at a fairground whilst in the army Motorcycle Display Team (1964)

At the army Physical Training College, Shorncliffe - back row, 2nd from right (1964)

Cutting the cake with Rosemary
at our wedding (1965)

My sister, Dawn, our
bridesmaid (1965)

Our daughter,
Maxine, aged
2 (1968)

Maxine, aged 3
with a panda that
I made (1969)

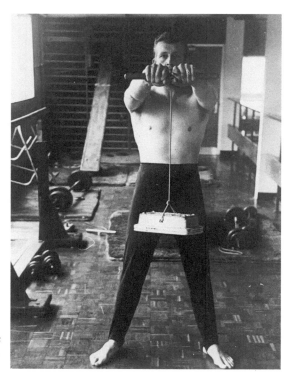

Keeping fit at Dean Close
School (1969)

Teaching at Dean Close School (1970)

Major Ben Chapman, my schoolteaching mentor at
Dean Close School, Cheltenham (1969)

On a trip with my fishing gear (1970)

A day fishing with Jeremy Wade when I broke the British carp fishing record by landing a quarter of a ton of carp in 24 hours (Bourton-on-the-Water, 1970)

With Dean Close boys at the Bisley Public School Shooting Championships (1971)

In Austria with Maxine on a
skiing trip a few months after her
mother, Rosemary, died (1972)

The 14th Century Priory at Kings Langley School where I lived
(1975-1986) with Maxine, and from 1981 also with my wife, Sarah

Catching a record carp
weighing over 35 lb
(Rickmansworth, 1977)

My father, aged 75 (1978)

Jeremy Wade
landing my carp at
Rickmansworth (1979)

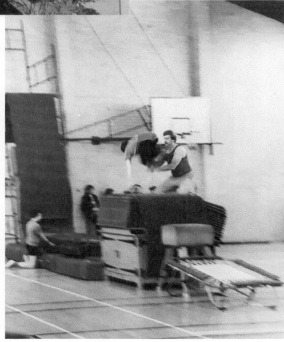

Teaching gym with
Maxine (1979)

Sarah and me at our wedding in Kings Langley (1981)

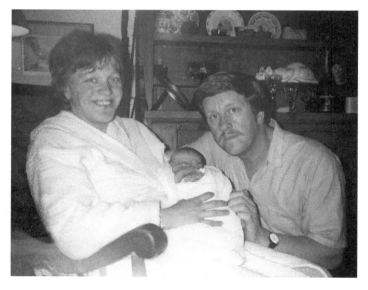

With Sarah and our first baby, William (1985)

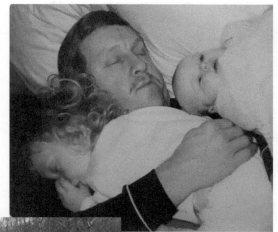

A nap with
William and baby
Natasha (1986)

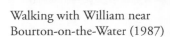

Walking with William near
Bourton-on-the-Water (1987)

Maxine in her early 20s

Sarah with
baby James
(1990)

With young James (1993)

Leading
an Acorn
expedition in
the Brecon
Beacons (1994)

Canoeing with
Acorn students
on the River
Wye during a
50 mile Paddle
and Survival
expedition (1994)

Sarah at home with
William, James, Natasha
and baby Oliver (1994)

Natasha's birthday party – me, James, Natasha, William, Sarah and Oliver (L to R) (1996)

Natasha, James, Sarah and Oliver (L to R) at Cotswold Water Park (1996)

Catching a 20 lb salmon in the River Spey, Scotland (2000)

With my good friend, Terry Oldfield, at home in Stroud (2001)

Steering our boat at Acorn Summer Camp (Cleddau Estuary, 2003)

Oliver wakeboarding at Cotswold Water Park (2006)

Archery at Acorn with young Barney (on left) who later became headteacher (2006)

An Acorn school play

Boat building
at Acorn

Acorn students coasteering
(St Davids, Pembrokeshire)

Acorn students coasteering
(St Davids, Pembrokeshire)

Oliver, William and James at Christmas (2010)

Oliver, James, Natasha, me, Sarah and William (L to R)
at Oliver's Acorn Graduation (2012)

Wedding of James and Emily at Chavenage House (L to R): Charlotte (Sarah's sister), Maxine, Oliver, Natasha, me, Emily, James, Sarah, William and Talia (2018)

Skiing with Natasha in Austria (2013)

Sarah (2020)

At Acorn with grandson, Leo, and our dog, Freida (2020)

With my granddaughter, Talia, and Maxine, at home (2021)

Playing my guitar at camp with Barney, Sarah and Acorn pupils (2021)

The Acorn School main building and
Barney (headteacher/gym teacher) (2022)

# CHAPTER 8

# PUBLIC SCHOOL TEACHING

On 16 June 1969 I walked quickly to my car, drove home, collected our pre-packed things and hit the road to Cheltenham.

I'd made a lucky escape from two controlling senior APTC WOs (warrant officers). I had done my best and had been a success but I'd been scarred, and for a few years I felt the pain of having been pushed around by dysfunctional unintelligent senior soldiers. I glanced at the Royal Military Police Training Depot as I drove past it on my way to freedom and felt relieved that I would no longer be browbeaten by the physical gods of the APTC.

With tears in my eyes, I chugged along with my wife and three-year-old child, breathing in the new fresh air of civilian life; the air that all those who were free of military control and might, breathed every day. I was floating on a cloud. I was free. I was on the road to change. What would become of me?

Seeking a new profession outside the army meant that my aims in trying to climb the military ladder were never fully realised. But thanks to the British Army, I emerged with a number of qualifications that easily enabled me to stand alongside the university graduates applying for teaching positions in public schools. I chose to continue my career in physical education, and with the additional courses I'd undertaken whilst in uniform, I was able to secure a schoolteaching post as Assistant to the Director of Physical Education at Dean Close School in Cheltenham.

Until the year I left the army, it wasn't clear to either me or Rosemary exactly what her family had done in keeping her Hodgkins diagnosis secret. Neither of us suspected that her illness was terminal, until she saw the word 'Hodgkins' on the flip chart at the bottom of her bed during one of her hospital stays. Although she was a psychiatric nurse, she knew little about the illness. I researched it at home using my medical books, and Rosemary also began to wonder about her prognosis. I finally explained the terminal nature of her Hodgkins lymphoma to her on the day I won my teaching post at Dean Close, having waited until she knew I had a safe job; and crucially, that she could receive chemotherapy in a leading treatment centre under the guidance of Professor Dr. Gamble, chief cancer specialist at Cheltenham General Hospital.

I didn't realise when I left the army that I would then be privileged to meet such a remarkable and inspiring man as Ben Chapman. The head of department, my new boss at Dean Close School, Major Benjamin David Chapman, DSO had coincidentally been a Warrant Officer in the APTC. He had been a war hero in Korea, and his citation states that Major Chapman crawled into a minefield to rescue several of his men, whilst apparently part naked. He also retrieved the bodies of those who were killed, carrying them out of the minefield.

Leaving the regular army and becoming a teacher at Dean Close didn't mark the complete end of my army career. Soon after stepping into civilian life, I joined the Territorial Army (TAVR) and was awarded the Queen's Commission, as 488963 Second Lieutenant Whiting in The Gloucestershire Regiment (1 Glosters). I also became the Training Officer in the school's Officer Training Corps, known then as the CCF, where Ben was my guide as a commissioned officer responsible for young boys, many of whom would eventually become officers in the three services.

Ben Chapman was a giant of a human being, not only because of his illustrious career as a war veteran, with a DSO (Distinguished Service Order) and a plethora of medals in the realm of physical education, particularly swimming and diving; but because he was a man of venerable stature, despite standing only five feet five inches tall.

He walked with a notable swagger, had a zest for smoking a pipe and in today's language you could call him 'super cool'. Ben taught me how to be a teacher. Despite my many years in the army, his charismatic and confident skills as my director meant that I would not be teaching his most able students until I was ready to honour them in the same way that he did; which is absolutely as it should be.

Ben didn't suffer fools gladly, and although he was aware of every frown, every face pulled and every comment from his teaching colleagues, he had his own distinctive views on everything. Working with him as his assistant during those years gave me an insight into a man of great talent and genius, not only in the physical realm but also in the human domain. I had learned to value the certifications in my career, but Ben taught me that the memories are far more important than the pieces of paper. He was not only my mentor; he was kind and caring on every level. Ben had the great gift of being able to embrace people he met with his expansive personality, and he certainly fathered me, trained me, taught me and helped my wife and daughter through some difficult times.

I treasure many delightful personal memories of Ben and we had a lot of fun together. Ben loved to joke and could tell really interesting anecdotes about his life in the army, embellishing what he said so skilfully that each element of the story seemed to be the truth. Every day in term time he would grace our gym office with such tales, sucking away at his Sherlock Holmes style pipe with its silver ring, while he entertained us with story after story. I have dined on many since, including the one about one of his men in Korea who had lost a testicle to shrapnel and had written to Ben the Christmas after the loss, to report that he was pleased to let Major Chapman know that he was sparking successfully on one cylinder! It took me some time to look past the exaggerations and identify what old soldiers do so well: hide the reality of pain and loss through contrived humour and a great deal of bullshit.

Having been a member of the army's gymnastics high-horse team and after performing in the Royal Tournament and the Edinburgh and Cardiff Tattoos as well as a number of military shows, I thought I could easily introduce my own way of doing things into the school's gymnastic lessons. But Ben always made sure that every lesson I taught was carefully prepared and planned, and he got me to try over and over again to get things right, inspecting each lesson plan and making sure he experienced and approved of my demonstrations. By 1970 I was allowed to do most of the lessons without his support, and provided what I planned was professional and appropriate, I was left to it.

I'd gained a bit of a reputation in the army for human pyramid building, and although Ben had also been engaged in these as a young Lance Corporal in 1939, I thought I could bring a newness to the lessons. I wanted to push the boundaries, using the skills I'd learned in the motorcycle display team in 1964, when we constructed pyramids of motorcycle riders. The main pyramid in which I rode involved five tiers of riders who wheeled around a field at just ten miles an hour, to ensure stability. Surely, we could get the boys at school to do the same thing, only without the motorbikes?

Many of our summertime lessons on Chapel Close involved building these human pyramids. The boys loved this activity and sometimes they even didn't fall! Ben used to run around the pyramids and check that every boy's arms were straight, backs were horizontal and muscles tensed to make a strong framework on which the top tiers could stand. It was a great lesson, and I still create the same pyramids at my school today, fifty years after Ben and I were doing them.

The trampoline was first constructed by Nissan from scrap metal in 1930, so it meant a great deal to have two of them at Dean Close, less than forty years after it was first invented. Ben and I were both trampolinists with national qualifications as trampoline coaches, so in the 1960s we were teaching and performing to a high level.

Ben, who was by then a most competent over-fifty-year-old trampolinist, had to usurp me whenever the two of us had a competition during our free lessons. How could I respond appropriately, taking on a man twenty-five years older than me when I could do almost every trick in the book? It was an easy call – I wanted to keep my job, so I made sure I lost!

Ben loved game shooting and came out with me a few times. He quickly fell in love with my old-fashioned English side-by-side double-barrelled twelve-bore and once shot a brace of woodcock with it, a right and a left. This was an extraordinary feat as you might only get one chance in a whole lifetime to have a shot at a single woodcock, let alone a pair flying side by side. After the kill, he turned to me as he swankily ejected the spent cartridges and with his usual wry smile, nonchalantly ran an oily cloth over the barrels and stood calmly waiting for the next bird.

Following the shoot that day, he mentioned that he loved the shotgun, so I gave it to him as a gift, only to find out later that it was a very valuable piece of equipment and worth a lot of money. I gently raised the subject in conversation and invited him on a shoot a month later, but he couldn't hit a single bird. No wonder – he had sawn four inches off the barrels and rendered the shotgun valueless; I pretended not to mind. I didn't know what a highly prized gun a Purdey was back then, and I did feel rather bereft when I found out its value; also a bit sad as the shotgun had been left to me by my father.

While Ben greatly inspired me, cared for me and taught me an immense amount about teaching children and life, he was also the world's most outrageous show-off. I remember once taking the school swimming team for training and executing some quite impressive dives from the 3-metre springboard, in order to encourage our up-and-coming senior diver. I had performed a few dives and was walking up the steps to get ready for another, when I glimpsed out of the corner of my eye, fifty-year-old Ben, a brief swimming costume bedecking his muscular, tanned body and a towel around his neck, walking to the poolside.

I performed a nice two and a half forward somersault piked, and when I surfaced I could see Ben standing on the balcony rail. From that slippery rail, he did the most perfect swallow dive I have ever seen. I didn't know until he died that Ben was the British Army diving champion during WWII and had a collection of impressive medals, some Olympic, which I'd seen many times, displayed in a mahogany case at his home.

On another occasion in late 1970, Ben and I were walking along the pebble beach at Selsey when a group of young men laughed at him. He was smoking his pipe rather nonchalantly and rose to their ridicule. He asked me to hold his pipe as he stood still on the pebbly beach in front of them. Ben gave them a knowing sideways glance and threw a hollow back somersault; the silence was golden.

While at Dean Close, I was able to continue to pursue my love of music. I bought an album of Leonard Cohen's songs, which motivated me to look at getting a new guitar and to widen my repertoire beyond numbers by Eric Burdon and The Animals and similar pop songs. In a music shop in Cheltenham, I found a shiny new Kimbara guitar made in Japan which looked so beautiful in its hard case that I couldn't resist buying it, together with a 'How to Play Classical Guitar' booklet.

I was fortunate to find a sixth form pupil, Jane Lachlan, to teach me and encourage me to eventually take classical guitar lessons. It was particularly meaningful to me to be inspired in my love of guitar by a pupil, and I owe her great gratitude. I am not a very proficient player, but I love folk guitar, and over the last fifty years I've taught a lot of young people to fall in love with the beauty and pleasure of playing the guitar.

Another pupil I got to know well was Jeremy Wade, a boy I met when he was just thirteen and who is now a well-known angler, freshwater detective, biologist, author and TV presenter. Jeremy attended my angling club at Dean Close, and in the summer holidays I used to take him and his friends on fun fishing expeditions to Norfolk. Jeremy was very much part of my enthusiasm for carp fishing at Dean Close and afterwards, and we have fished together in many rivers and lakes in Norfolk, Suffolk and Gloucestershire.

I remember he could fall asleep anywhere, including on top of a pile of bags and rods, in the narrow gap between the kit and the roof of my car, with his face pressed upside down against the back window! But when Jeremy woke, he was the most successful of anglers, able to catch the biggest fish. We are still good friends, and I know that since that time he has gone on to catch snakes and once even caught a caiman which was chasing him down the Amazon. I like to think that some of his appetite for adventuring was sparked by the sense of being wild explorers that we enjoyed on our fishing trips.

Ben was understanding when he heard about my wife's illness and allowed me to take the necessary days off. I was aware, as a father of a young child and with an ill wife, that my job was at risk; especially as I had to spend so much time away from school, often nipping home in my MG to look after Rosemary and prepare the house for her to be able to care for Maxine when she came home from school. It was a hard time for Rosemary; and for me, having to care for a wife and child and hold down a full-time job at the same time.

Rosemary was brave and beautiful throughout the time she was afflicted with the disease that she came to understand would eventually end her life. I was determined to keep Rosemary's illness from Maxine and did all I could to excuse obvious things such as mood swings and the rapidly changing physical appearance of one so ill. Maxine was my main concern, for by a certain point I knew that Rosemary only had a short time left. The endless months and years of sleeplessness, of trying to keep house and be a constant carer for Rosemary as well as an attentive father while holding down a demanding full-time position, was all extremely difficult to manage; but I accepted that this was my lot in life, and I'm pleased that by the grace of God, I was able to cope as well as I did.

I had many daily tasks, such as getting Rosemary out of bed in the middle of the night, while Maxine slept, and laying her in a bath of warm water as she scrubbed her itching body – one of the main symptoms of lymphatic cancer, Hodgkin's lymphoma. She would scratch and scratch until some of her skin fell off into the bath. After these ritual baths I would let the water out, and when it was gone I would dry Rosemary's poor, scratched body and lift her out of the bath. A silk sheet was draped over a bed in the spare room ready to lay her down, and then I'd cover her body with the Calamine lotion that seemed to give her some comfort. Within an hour or so, Rosemary would be ready to slip on her silk nightie and get back into bed, absolutely exhausted but never complaining. This was a nightly ritual throughout 1971 and 1972, and I did my best to keep it from Maxine. Rosemary needed so many medications and lotions that were not supplied by the NHS that I had to take on a part-time job to pay for them.

I went to school each day absolutely shattered. But one thing the army had taught me was that a soldier can overcome anything, so I was able to snap out of this continual tiredness and teach. I could at least look forward to going to bed at seven most nights after I'd read Maxine's story, whilst Rosemary, exhausted, itching and worried, struggled to fall asleep. If she had not taken to her bed so early, she would never have had the strength to get through her days.


During my time at the school, I encouraged, guided and helped develop The Sandhurst Platoon, so called because all its members either had aspirations to attend Sandhurst, or aligned interests. This initiative offered those young students who wished to become officers in the army, a window into army life before making the commitment to a military future. It was started in 1970, led by pupil Peter Marks, and grew from activities in the

Duke of Edinburgh's Scheme, with all of its members attaining Silver or Gold. The exploits of the group were legendary, involving expeditions and camps on which skills in map reading, wild camping, canoeing, fishing, trapping, skinning and cooking on open fires were put into practice. I loved those days of fun and adventure and am happy to still be connected to many of those who participated fifty years ago.

I also remember the headteacher at that time with great affection. Christopher Turner was an excellent role model, much appreciated by his staff. He was an upright, moral, towering figure with strong Christian values which he demonstrated every day at the school. I felt privileged to have lunch several times in his private dining room with the chosen few. His leadership skills were immense, but I don't think he really appreciated how great a man and admirable headteacher he was. He is now a retired vicar, and a recent visit to my home in the Cotswolds with his wife, Lucia, confirmed the grace of the man in his later life.

Ben Chapman died at the age of ninety-three. I owe Ben for giving me my skill as a physical educationist. I've always had a naturally high level of energy, with an abundance of enthusiasm and exuberance. This, together with a quick, independent mind and an irrepressible urge to challenge certain norms, has taken me to some wonderful places with some extraordinary people; and also tended to land me in trouble. I've learnt that these qualities can be admired by some and abhorred by others. In Ben, I was lucky to find someone who shared my ideals, and who matched my energy and encouraged me in finding the best ways to channel it. I loved and respected that man like no other except for my father, and I know he loved me like a son; although at times he made my life a misery by always trying to beat me on the trampoline!

My last clear memory of Dean Close School is when I heard early on the morning of 16 June 1972 that Rosemary had passed away at her mother's house. I had left her with her mother for a week, and Maxine was with her aunt, whilst I organised the school's commemoration activities. Fortunately, I was allowed to travel to Suffolk to my mother-in-law's home to be with Maxine after her brave mother died, finally relieved of the great pain she had endured for so long without complaint.

That drive was a hard one. Would Rosemary still be where she had died? Would Maxine know? What arrangements had been made so far? I drove fast, crying much of the journey and wishing I had been at Rosemary's side when she died. But inside, I felt a great relief because her suffering had ended. Though now, what of Maxine and her life?

On arriving at the house, it was clear that Maxine didn't know, so I put her in the car and drove out of the town. When I told her, she was terribly upset, and I had to hold back my pain as I nursed her in my arms. She cried on and off for days, but somehow she came to terms with it rather more quickly than I could have hoped. I think, mainly because I'd protected her from the difficult periods, and she didn't really understand what had happened.

I left Maxine with her aunt for the funeral, which was a grand affair. John Wade, Jeremy's father, was the vicar of Nayland, and he was very helpful to me during this terrible time. The streets of Nayland were lined with villagers who walked behind the coffin with great respect for 'Frikey', the girl with the Irish eyes. My old school friend, Colin, sympathetically and nobly attended to give me support, which meant a great deal. Rosemary's family had their own private plot in the Catholic cemetery, where she was laid to rest with her father. She was just twenty-seven years old; what a loss.

# CHAPTER 9

# CYPRUS AND A BIG LESSON

Within a year of Rosemary's passing, I had met another woman and was about to learn a huge lesson.

This beautiful, intelligent, professional older woman was not what she appeared to be, and of course, in time the extent of her deception was revealed. I have had to work hard to forgive and forget, and it has taken until recently for me to fully appraise what happened.

I met Carole in 1973 and was swept off my feet by this lady who also appeared to have fallen for me. She seemed immediately fond of Maxine and filled my head with all kinds of exciting ideas about what we could do if we were together, saying that Maxine would be the centre of her new plans and that she wanted to be her loving mother.

I can now see that I was being wooed and that Carole wanted to trail me along to meet her affluent intellectual friends in Hampstead in order to show off her new, young conquest. But at the time, I just seemed to be spinning without a centre, infatuated by all she had to offer. After so many years of nursing Rosemary, who had had no energy for any show of love or warmth towards me, and struggling to care for her and Maxine whilst working full-time, meeting Carole was almost like being reborn.

We attended Mensa (the high IQ society) sessions and often wrote poetry together. I was becoming more confident about my work in education and was invited by an academic group that was an offshoot of Mensa, to give a talk about my childhood and path to adult life. What I spoke about regarding my own schooling was that my teachers merely saw me as a poor waif and didn't try to find the human being that was inside the 'war child' standing in front of them. Education at that time wouldn't allow teachers to see the individual behind the outer image of poverty. I wondered what I would have become had my teachers found the inner being inside the outer form and taught me in a way that enabled my hidden capabilities to be embraced and brought to life. I suggested that education needed to move away from competition and towards child-centred ways of teaching that would enable all children to develop their true potential. It was encouraging to be accepted in an academic setting and to be able to reveal the golden vision of education that had been quietly maturing inside me since I was that skinny boy being chastised on stage in front of the whole school. It must have touched something in the audience, because after my brief presentation I was aware that many of the group were in tears.

Carole had told me that she was a professional writer, could speak seven languages and had a PhD in philosophy. She was the author of many books, Professor of Languages at Perugia University and also wrote for a national newspaper. She had bought her own house in Hampstead which, she explained, we could let out for a small fortune to enable the three of us to live a life of travel. At the time, it sounded enticing.

I was somewhat glazed and more and more sucked in by this new woman in my life. Her first husband was actually a very successful academic and when I met him once, he seemed like a fine man. But the twinkle in his eye and a few sideways looks were surely telling me something? Sadly, I didn't read his warning signals.

The year I left the army and went into public school education, I'd bought a detached four-bedroom house in Tewkesbury to give the family some security. I'd also managed to earn and save a great deal of money whilst teaching at Dean Close. For a time, thanks to the generosity and goodwill of the school, Maxine had almost lived in my school study, just coming home with me to sleep. Then before her mother died, Maxine had started boarding at the school, giving her the security of a first-class private school with many friends and a great school life, all of which were paramount. This enabled me to have a number of part-time jobs outside of school hours, so I filled my spare time with making more money. My varied pursuits included working as a personal trainer, a fitness instructor, a bricklayer and a digger on building sites.

With hindsight, it's obvious to me now that I completely fell for Carole's carefully laid trap. Within a few months of meeting her I had resigned my job, sold my house and made plans to travel to the Middle East with her and Maxine. What kind of fool was I? But it all seemed so exciting after those many difficult years.

Whenever Carole and I talked about money, she was quick to tell me not to worry, that we would have a luxurious life funded by the rental income from her house, and that she would be the banker in our relationship and take care of the finances so that I wouldn't need to worry. I was too quick to agree to being relieved of all financial responsibility, and she took me to the bank, unfortunately not kicking and screaming. We signed up for a joint account with only one signatory necessary for any transaction, and due to my naïvety, no alarm bells rang.

Everything seemed to fit into place, and at Carole's insistence, within a few months I was married again for the second time. I was looking forward to being with this new woman who promised to take care of me and to love me and my darling daughter, wiping away all our troubled years.

After the wedding the three of us travelled across Europe and boarded a ship in Venice to sail around the Greek islands. On arriving in the southern port of Limassol, Cyprus, we took a taxi to Kyrenia where I had served in 1964, and I rekindled some Greek friendships.

A man I met in a café introduced me to a local businessman who sold us a detached three-bedroom house built on pillars, with sixteen acres of orange and lemon trees, a sprinkling of pomegranate trees, and more grapevines than one would ever need for a winery. When I asked Carole how we'd paid for the house, she was quick to assure me that it was chicken feed compared to the money we had between us.

I swapped my grapes and fruit for car servicing, cleaning, a maid and as much petrol as I could use. I got the worst end of the deal but couldn't have cared less. I was content, and Maxine enjoyed her new private school and blissfully swimming in the Mediterranean every morning under the warm Cyprus sun. Carole never went into the water, though, as she always stayed at home to protect her costly wigs!

We were all happy and life was generally easy, except for one notable incident when I rescued a very large gentleman from an airbed that had drifted out to sea. He was screaming and so was the crowd lining the beach, but there was no lifeguard so I dived into the waves. It took me over an hour to swim out and reach him, and when I did, he panicked and struggled, kicking me in the face and breaking my nose and three teeth. After swallowing my teeth and hitting him hard to stun him, which was the only way I could calm him down, I paddled for two hours to bring him back to shore to the waiting ambulance. We shook hands and I went home with three gaps instead of my teeth.

Soon after we moved into our new house, I started a school in the village. It was popular with the locals and well attended by children from the surrounding area. About five hundred pupils, up to age sixteen, would come to the village square every day to be taught by me and a handful of backpackers from Australia and New Zealand who were keen to help. I was mostly paid in wine! We had plans to build a new school, but that didn't come to fruition because of what happened next, which led me to withdraw from the project.

After we'd been in Cyprus for a few weeks I opened a letter addressed to Mr and Mrs Whiting and discovered that, without my knowledge,

Carole had enrolled Maxine as a boarder at Cheltenham Ladies College. I was shocked and horrified and tore the letter up as there was no way my new wife could ever expect me to ditch my beloved daughter. Our house was lovely, the sun shone, the sea was an opalescent turquoise green, and in our idyllic life we could walk there in two minutes. But something was wrong. Following receipt of that letter, my heart went out of our Cyprus existence, and a cautionary event was soon to change everything.

Maxine always came into our bedroom at about six each morning for a cuddle with me. One July morning when the hot weather was becoming unbearable, we stood on the balcony gazing out at our new estate and saw a long black snake move from the base of an orange tree and powerfully wriggle across the garden. Maxine screamed and the snake must have sensed the vibration as it disappeared down a hole. It was gone, but where would it be at night, and how many of them were in the orange grove?

I was shaken and began to wonder that day whether snakes eat oranges and lemons, was our cheap house on stilts for a reason, and were rats eating the fruit and snakes eating the rats? What had we bought?

After a sleepless night, I went to see our groundsman and indicated to him that we'd seen a snake, upon which he smiled and lifted his trousers to show me his lower legs covered with marks from old snake bites. Apparently, after a lifetime of being bitten, he assured us he was now immune to their poison. But that was of no help to us. And in the local cafe, my worst fears were confirmed – we had bought the house that, for good reason, nobody else wanted.

We were absolutely stunned and straight away made plans to move to Kyrenia. The next day Carole decided we should get a new car to better suit our upgraded wealthy lifestyle, and we bought an automatic 3.8 litre Jaguar, white with red leather seats. It was like driving on a magic carpet of silk. As usual, Carole handled the payment and told me it was paid for from her private account as a gift to me.

However, at that point some political trouble was brewing in Cyprus, so we decided it would be best to leave the island. We had a house with a snake-infested garden to sell and a Jaguar to dispose of.

One morning I went under the house to open the car doors to air the inside and sat in the driver's seat admiring the walnut dashboard with its beautiful instruments. I was wondering how we would get out of this situation, how much money had gone from my account and how much was left, when I heard a hiss behind me, and on the back seat I saw a huge angry black snake. Using a long stick, I was luckily able to encourage it to leave the car and wriggle down a hole in the garden, just before we had a house viewing.

We sold the house to an English holidaymaker for £1,700, losing almost a quarter of what we'd paid. I did warn him about the snakes, but all he said was, 'Oh, I like snakes!' In the meantime, we stayed in the Hotel Adonis, on the harbour at Kyrenia. Next was the car, which belonged to Carole, and that was easily sold to someone who had been admiring it. We landed back in England and initially went to a hotel. I was anxious to see my family and to reunite Maxine with her relatives.

During the summer break while Maxine was with family, I had a brief and rather unusual adventure in France, working in a French circus just outside Fontainebleau. I undertook the task out of regard for a few people to whom I'd taught some acrobatic gymnastics, and because of the irresistible financial reward that was offered. The circus was in difficulty as their strongman had died, and they needed to find a temporary replacement as quickly as possible. I hotfooted it over the channel, and although I was only half his size, I stood in for the old strongman, using my army nickname of 'Tiger'. I performed stunts such as blowing up hot water bottles and pulling heavy weights with my then long hair. I quickly made a lot of money, but opted out and returned home after a couple of weeks as I wasn't enjoying circus life and found the way they mistreated the animals too upsetting.

Another unusual extra-curricular activity that year was the annual telephone directory tearing up competition. I entered just for fun and broke the British record by managing to tear up seven directories in a minute – all I can say is that there's a knack to it!

In September 1973 we moved to Croydon and I secured a position as Head of Physical Education and Outdoor Pursuits at a public school. My salary was double what was advertised, as I had to create a new department. I worked hard, but sadly all was not well with the school. It became clear that some of the rugby team staff were more interested in the showering after the match than in the actual game; a more senior master wanted me to go home while he supervised the showers. I soon found another, better post in Surrey at an independent school. That seemed a sensible move after Cyprus, and there was also a good school for Maxine. I loved my new job, and all seemed well.

For some reason, Carole had to go to her house in Hampstead one day, and because she couldn't drive, she called a taxi. Meanwhile, I drove to school in my new Ferrari Dino – apparently another generous gift from my wife. Later that morning a housemaster told me that he liked my wife's new car. He had seen her in a Bentley Continental, driven by an old man with a beard.

Hearing this, my mind went into overdrive, and I was suddenly brought to my senses. I asked the headteacher if I could leave school early and went home. Maxine was still at school, and for the first time I had the house to myself. My mother-in-law, Carole's mother, called me to ask for the details of her daughter's bank account. I wasn't sure where they were, so I told her I would look and call her when I'd found them.

I knew that my new wife was very secretive and had a locked drawer in my study for her private things. Keen to help my mother-in-law, I managed to open the drawer, and what I found was to change my life. In the drawer were bank statements neatly packed into an envelope, both joint and Carole's own specific private account, a building society book, lots of receipts and boxes of expensive bespoke black wigs.

I discovered that the things we had bought, air fares, hotels, taxis, restaurant bills, the Cyprus house, the Jaguar, the Ferrari etc, had all been paid for out of our joint account. And when I saw that the balance had fallen from many thousands to less than £800, I realised I had been scammed and had paid for everything since we'd met. There were also several receipts for large amounts of money transferred from my account to Carole's building society account, while no money had been transferred from her accounts to our joint account.

My darling, lovable and loving wife had stolen almost every penny I had earned, and her private bank statement showed that almost nothing had been withdrawn from her account for almost a year. Each month there was a payment into her private building society account for rent from the Hampstead house. The savings in her private bank account plus the even larger amount in her building society account, on top of the value of her Hampstead house, would total several millions in today's money.

During our brief relationship Carole had used up all the money I'd received from the house in Tewkesbury and the cars and everything else. I had been ripped off, and the many bills for her dresses, jewellery, wigs, shoes, subscriptions to organisations and donations to members of her family all told the story; but they were carefully hidden between the pages of a book on our bookshelf. Carole had secreted them inside James Joyce's 'Ulysses' which she knew I had already read, so she thought they would be safe from discovery.

I realised that the ride in the Bentley also needed to be questioned. I bided my time and after supper that night, I told Carole she'd been seen in a Bentley driven by an old man. She just looked straight at me, told a raft of lies whilst shedding a few crocodile tears and said she was sorry. But there was no way I could accept any of her fabrications. I had been a fool, a bloody fool.

The next day I drove Carole to her luxurious house in Hampstead and parked her in her friend's sitting room. She sat crying, whilst still lying through her teeth. She declared she was broken, though it soon became clear that this was all planned, and it taught me a real lesson. Carole was not the loving woman I thought I had married, but an accomplished actress and a brazen liar on a grand scale.

I divorced her, and with no children between us, the story ended. Sadly, for some months she wrote me love letters and called me with all kinds of stories, clearly in a disturbed frame of mind. Carole never remarried and according to her closest friend, she regretted what she had done for the rest of her life, until her death in 2013.

The man in the Bentley turned out to be a wealthy art dealer who had bought Carole the Hampstead house some years before. He was titled and in his eighties, and two weeks after she had been despatched to Hampstead I called at his nearby house.

I wanted to put the whole affair to bed and understand what had happened during that year, and we had a heart-to-heart. He was a nice but lonely man, who told me he gave Carole an allowance and had bought her the house in Hampstead as a gift when she was younger. He said that he'd become depressed when Carole had fallen for a younger man and that he loved her and would do anything for her. He was pushed aside because I was more than fifty years his junior, and he couldn't compete. So, using the promise of his wealth, he persuaded her to deceive me with apparently platonic visits while I was at school.

That chapter was finally closed, and I had learned a hard lesson.

# CHAPTER 10

# STEINER TEACHING AND SARAH

An incident occurred in December 1974 with an aftermath the following year. One afternoon I decided to drive to London to do my Christmas shopping, leaving Maxine with a friend in Surbiton. I was full of enthusiasm for the gift I planned to buy her – a china doll costing £20 that I'd seen on my last visit to Hamley's in Oxford Street.

It was getting dark, and after parking on the outskirts I started walking briskly towards the centre. On the way, I passed an elderly couple coming up out of the Underground who advised me not to walk under the bypass. They suggested I'd best find another route because there was a gang of yobs down there waiting to rob any unsuspecting pedestrians. They explained that they'd been lucky, telling me,

'They let us pass because we're old.'

I felt it behoved me, as an ex army police officer, to be willing to engage with any gang that frightened older people or threatened their right to go about their business without fear. I'd been trained to carry out a citizen's arrest if the public were in danger and knew there was little risk to my safety due to my military martial arts training. So I took the steps down towards the underpass and soon came upon the group, their ear-splitting noise echoing through the tunnel. They were chatting, shouting, arguing, being silly, playing around with beer bottles and staggering about on the broken glass which littered their patch. I walked on, to one side of them, and greeted them with my usual polite,

'Hi guys.' But they were out for a fight and the half dozen of them all stepped across, blocking my way:

'Turn out your pockets. Give us what you've got and we'll let you pass.'

I recalled the many times I'd had to deal with such violent groups when I was an MP in the army, and I didn't want to harm them as they were just teenagers trying to be tough. But they clearly wanted trouble. Their ringleader stood out, big and evil-looking, and one of his cohorts urged him to,

'Give 'im a smackin', Kev. Teach 'im a lesson!'

Kevin stood in front of me, wielding a large brown bottle, and it was clear he wanted the money he assumed was in my pocket. I peeled off a £1 note from the wad I was carrying and offered it to him. But that wasn't enough, he wanted it all, so I refused and stood my ground.

One of the gang said,

'You don't know who you're dealing with, mate. We're the Hendon mob. We eat people like you.'

That was it! My usual approach of talking myself out of a bad situation by being humble and letting the other side feel victorious, hadn't worked, and I could either be bashed about by the gang and perhaps seriously injured, or take action. So I did what I could do best, parried the attack and took the broken bottle out of Kevin's hand, then dropped the knife bearer, removed his knife and dealt with him. Only three of the gang stayed, and all three quickly ended up lying on the ground in front of me amongst the broken glass, bleeding and clearly hurt, while the others ran away, shouting. I'd had no choice but to inflict some hard blows and defensive actions on them, and I attended to their injuries while waiting for someone to call an ambulance and the police.

I helped them up, gave them a brief chat about their behaviour and reminded them that I'd not wanted to hurt them. They were clearly shocked and upset. A couple of policemen arrived on the scene and seeing the three injured bodies, assumed they had been assaulted and I was the culprit! I was handcuffed, while the three miscreants shouted that I had attacked them. I asked one of the policemen to take my identification out of my wallet, and when they saw that I was an ex-policeman and a deputy headteacher, things took a different turn. The cuffs were removed, the three were arrested, and we were all taken to the local police station where I was praised and asked whether I wanted to press charges, which I declined.

I sent a message to the three boys in their cells, telling them to speak the truth and that since they were injured and I was unharmed, I wouldn't press charges against them. That seemed to elicit a change of attitude, and they were just put on police watch for a year. I discovered they were already known to the police, and apparently two of the gang told the true story, exonerating me from any wrongdoing.

The next episode was unexpected. At that time, Maxine was madly enthusiastic about the trampoline, and I was offering trampoline lessons in the evenings to a variety of ages, including older teenagers. In June the following year, six youngsters stood in the doorway of the hall where I was teaching, and I instantly recognised one of them as Kevin, the young man who'd wanted to cut me up with a bottle. I asked them what they wanted and Kevin said,

'Not another beasting, mate, I can't go through that again!'

I taught three of them trampolining, and they became regulars until the following Christmas, taking the tube all the way from Hendon to Kingston-on-Thames and then walking to Surbiton for our sessions. I'm sure we all learned a lesson, and meeting these young men helped to reinforce my view that there is a golden light of potential shining inside everyone, no matter what they look like and how they behave.

That year, I applied for several positions in major public schools. The few interviews I was offered tied my stomach in knots because, given my experience, I was often one of the preferred candidates – but partly due to my older sister Kim's encouragement, I was tending to favour a move away from public school. Since I began teaching, Kim and I had often shared our thoughts on education, and we had many views in common about the ways in which education needed to develop in order for children's needs to be truly met. Kim had set up her own Montessori school in London, and as my daughter's welfare was my main priority, Kim recommended that I enter Steiner education in order to give Maxine a child-centred education that encouraged free thinking.

The Rudolf Steiner school at Kings Langley in Hertfordshire was a boarding school built on the foundations of an old royal palace with a fourteenth century priory next door where some of the teachers lived. It was very different from Dean Close, and I was initially alarmed when I attended the interview, as I was interviewed by about thirty rather relaxed and unusual people. One of the interviewers commented on my three-piece tweed suit and brown trilby, the common headgear of retired soldiers, and I certainly stood out amongst the corduroy clad group of teachers. Nonetheless, I was offered the post.

However, when we discussed the salary I had a nasty shock. The bursar told me that working at the school was about commitment and not about money – and it turned out that the monthly sum being offered was less than the expenses I had been paid at my previous independent school in Surbiton. I left the meeting feeling rather deflated and wishing that I hadn't gone to the interview. As I was driving out of the school grounds, I saw a young pupil standing at the gate who looked rather troubled. She asked who I was and then said:

'I hope you come to the school because the gym is boring, and we do just about nothing. Fat girls like me get no help at all, not even to lose weight. Please come to the school! Please – we need you!'

Moved by her entreaty, I turned around and went back into the school office to accept the position with its meagre salary. For my living quarters, I was offered a small room in the priory plus a cupboard underneath the stairs leading up to the chapel and was told that this was the only available space for me and Maxine. I was able, though, to make a cosy home for us both in that room and the tiny area under the stairs, and we lived there together for the next six years.

One added benefit of my new job and living arrangements was that I was finally able to entertain my love of dogs, and Maxine and I got a sweet spaniel who we called Ben. During the twelve years I taught at Kings Langley we later had Jasper and then Jess, both black Labradors and congenial companions who were a continual source of comfort and delight.

Joining this school in 1975 was truly a saving grace for both me and Maxine who was by then nine; me after losing my young wife and Maxine after losing her mother – and both of us after having been through the previous unfortunate episode with Carole. At Kings Langley, I was delighted to be given the opportunity to develop my own system of physical education, putting into place all the experience I had gained from working in the army and public school. From 1972 I'd been a single parent, and when I came to this new school, I really had to step up and make sure I could look after Maxine as well as hold down an exciting and challenging new job.

Later that same year, I was walking into a pub one day when I bumped into a woman who asked me if I would teach the guitar to her nineteen-year-old daughter, Sarah, who was studying for an art degree at Watford College of Art. I agreed, and we soon started our guitar lessons. By about the fourth class we realised that we got on exceptionally well and really liked each other; but Sarah was my pupil, she was younger than me, and I also had a girlfriend, so there was no question of any romance. In the meantime, one of my teaching colleagues told me that he was attracted to Sarah and had asked her out on a date in the New Year to a performance at

The Royal Theatre in Windsor, which was actually then owned by Sarah's family. He wanted some help to smarten himself up for the outing, so I drove him up to London to get kitted out with a new suit.

On New Year's Eve a friend of mine, musician Martin Kershaw, invited me to a party in London that was going to be attended by some well-known people in the pop world. Driving down the road past her house on my way there, however, I was struck by a sudden realisation – I loved Sarah! I straight away pulled up to the house, and ran inside to talk to her. On hearing where I was going, Sarah's mother suggested that I take Sarah with me to the party. Sarah agreed and quickly got herself ready, looking like a million dollars, to come with me in my Jaguar and see in the New Year with Cliff Richard and friends.

The day after the party, New Year's day, I took Sarah to a country pub and despite my feelings, told her that we couldn't be together as I knew my colleague had already asked her out. But Sarah said it was too late, she'd already fallen for me and was cancelling her date! My colleague didn't talk to me for a year, but my relationship with Sarah went from strength to strength. Sarah and I agreed on a long old-fashioned courtship. And since she was younger and I was thirty, I suggested that we needed to court for at least six years before making any formal commitment, so that she could mature and grow into an independent young woman who knew what she was getting herself into before taking such a serious step. I was aware also, that it was important for Maxine to be old enough to understand that I could be ready for a new marriage.

From the beginning of our relationship, at the age of nineteen, Sarah became the most caring and devoted mother to my daughter, always putting Maxine's needs first and mothering her in the most loving way. Sarah and I didn't actually live together until we were married in 1981, when Maxine was sixteen, but throughout our six years of courting we really enjoyed our time together. We danced, walked, talked, played guitar, went to gym clubs and the theatre and generally delighted in each other's company. Sarah is a fine artist, loves singing, drama, crafts and nature, takes a sensitive holistic approach to life and has a tender, yet strong, heart. So being with her was, and still is, a joy and an inspiration.

Sarah's talented parents were involved in education and the film industry, and thankfully they were supportive of our being together. Her father was British film production designer, Michael Stringer, who became a close friend and my father-in-law. He was a distinguished man who had been a glider pilot at Arnhem during the war and was shot down and rescued by the French underground. Sarah's mother, Anne Stringer, was a gifted artist who designed some of Margot Fonteyn's headdresses. Her family owned Rydal Mount in the Lake District, home of William Wordsworth.

After a few months, Sarah decided to opt out of her art degree and asked me to train her as a gym teacher. I was then thrilled to be able to work with her as my assistant. The young Miss Stringer was a competent and popular gym instructor, much appreciated by the children, and we taught together side by side and day after day, for the next six years.

Sarah clearly recognised our shared vocation in teaching. Soon after we got together, my musician friend, Martin, offered me various exciting-sounding roles working with him, for example running a country hotel or being a road manager for touring bands. Although they were not worlds I was naturally drawn to, I might have been lured in one of those directions, as many inducements were offered – not least a pink Cadillac! But Sarah was sure that all of them would have been wrong for me and that my gift and destiny was to be a teacher. She was right, and I'm so grateful to her for her wisdom and clarity at that young age.

During our early days together, we did embark on one highly time con-suming diversion from teaching. In the early 1970s I had made some bespoke fishing rods for friends, and on one occasion I proudly produced a split-cane thirteen feet six inches salmon fly rod for a lady in Guiting Power who fished with the Queen Mother. Each time I visited her stately

Cotswold home with its beautiful lake in the extensive grounds, I was greeted by a butler who took me into the drawing room where she kept her rods and equipment in stylish leather trunks, ready for her winter fishing trip to the River Tweed in Scotland. I'd also noticed a large basket in the boot of her Rolls that I imagined to be full of wine and fine foods for her time away; I so wanted to go with her.

To make her the best possible rod, I'd bought the appropriate bamboo, split it myself and built a hexagonal fly rod exactly to her specifications, presenting it to her in a handmade walnut case lined with green baize. We walked down to the lake where I fitted her Hardy Perfect fly reel onto the rod, and she tied a Jock Scott, her favourite tube fly, onto the end of the leader. I was so anxious as to how the rod would perform, but then equally relieved when her face lit up as the fly line arched out towards the lake with a perfect action.

She paid me generously for the rod and commented on its exceptional quality, which encouraged me to consider her suggestion that I should make salmon rods for a living. Within a couple of years, I'd created a cottage industry employing a few local people who I trained to make specialised rods for fly and carp fishing. After a short time, the rods were in angling shops throughout London and Hertfordshire, and we had so many orders that our small workforce couldn't keep up with the necessary production. One of the salesmen kept advising me that I needed to expand the operation, and indeed, by 1978, The East Anglian Rod Company, run by Julian Pardoe, was asking for thousands of the various types of rods that I had designed.

Sarah and I were both working flat out making rods for these huge orders, and I was also selling them in Holland and elsewhere, travelling long distances while continuing to teach. I registered the business at Companies House as Dynaflex Tackle Limited. Each of our rods was given a specific name – The Tiger, The Ranger, The Miracle, The Stalker – and a set of trout fly rods was called The Church Hill Gold. I was amazed at the enthusiastic response to my designs so I took out a Registered Design Patent to try and protect them from being copied.

But within a couple of years of that registration, the market was flooded with copies, and I decided to break from my business partner and bring my focus fully back to teaching. Sarah supported this move as, alongside our teaching, we were working on the rods every evening and at weekends – something had to give. Besides, I was upset that people were copying my rods, and at that time we couldn't afford to permanently register the designs nationwide. I became disillusioned with the angling manufacturing world, and in 1979 I finally wound up the business. Unfortunately, at the end of this episode I was left with a debt plus hundreds of sets of rod-building materials which were difficult to sell. Dynaflex had quickly turned from a fun, exciting and creative adventure into an onerous commercial undertaking, and so it ended up as only a short-lived distraction from our teaching careers.

In that era there was a lot of enthusiasm for carp fishing, and I continued pursuing my love of angling. I would often go on expeditions to a lake near Norwich together with my oldest brother, Bill, and a friend called Dennis. We would camp in a forest where we honed our equipment and prepared the new float fishing system that I'd designed to catch the big ones. We were so keen to get in early, that we'd set up a temporary base by the lake and wait until midnight for the opening of the new angling season. It was difficult to resist casting an early line as we could hear the fish clooping and swirling in the water. Earlier in the day, I would climb up a tree, binoculars in hand, to look down on the formidable and ancient creatures of the lake. We enjoyed such glorious and exciting times on our trips.

One year we went off to the lake as usual, the day before the start of the angling season. Looking into the water, I saw a large majestic carp confidently cruising through the water, followed by a school of followers, all copying her every move. She was a female with a huge belly full of spawn and looked to be a great weight. In eager anticipation, we took our rods down to the lake early the next morning and were surprised to see no other anglers around. Why would such a superb lake be devoid of anglers? It seemed rather eerie, but we were delighted to be the only ones ready for the off.

I sat under the tree I'd climbed beforehand and watched the dawn breaking, like a veil drawn by the rising sun to reveal the lake. I saw a set of bubbles steadily rising and, plotting its route through the water, knew it was a carp. I threaded a few more wriggling worms onto my hook and flicked the bait into the water where I thought the fish would be. Almost straight away, the float shivered and vibrated and then I felt the carp bite. The fish shot from underneath the trees towards the far end of the lake, bending my rod down almost horizontally, and we fought for about fifteen minutes before it finally gave up, and I was able to slip my net beneath it.

When I landed the carp and laid it on the soft grass, I wanted to hold and applaud my catch. It seemed like a salutation to honour her by admiring her beautiful body, lit by the early morning rising sun. As I held her, the boys poured water on her to clean off the bits of grass, and then they photographed us. I could see she weighed well over 30 lbs. I slipped her back into the lake, and we were all thrilled with such a catch on the first day of the season on a lake with no other anglers. How lucky we felt.

Later on when we'd just finished our snacks, the bailiff appeared in his truck, and we gave him a cuppa. He was, as always, kind and interested in our plans. And then came the shock.

'Well boys, I expect you're waiting for the season to begin at midnight. Not long to wait and I hear there are a lot of big carp moving. I know many anglers will be arriving this afternoon, keen to get the best swims. Len will be after the big one he's been watching for the past week.'

'Wow,' said Dennis. 'Is it really big?'

'When it comes out it will be a new Norfolk record, I can assure you,' replied George.

We looked at one another and realised that we'd got the dates wrong and our huge record-breaking carp had been caught the day before the season opened! Gutted by this, but still elated by our achievement, we fished on for the rest of the week, listening to all the other anglers talking endlessly about a huge fish that was often seen rolling and clooping at night.

In my spare time, as well as writing articles on fishing for fishing magazines, I wrote some poetry that I submitted to various publications:

The Fisher's World

Gently rolling hills, silver streams through valleys dart,
Like tinsel stretching their substance to the sea.
Appealing lakes hidden like nests amidst all this beauty,
Leaves seemingly waving like fans silently cooling deeps and
shallows.
Flat calm sheets of silver, gently dimpled by creatures from below,
In strivings for sustenance,
Darting shapes armoured like forts, roaming unendingly.

Roach, rudd and perch in shoals of kind,
Swaying gracefully in rhythmic movement hypnotising the
unnoticed watcher.
Pike with evil malicious faces stalking, catching innocent prey,
Chewing, crunching tiny bodies for his own satisfaction,
Not knowing why nature gave it such a disposition.
Eels writhing, sliding, wriggling in mud,
Cleaning soulless bodies from the deep lakes' bed.

Lurking carp with faces of angels, dorsal fins like sails,
Dark backs and huge scales like halos shining,
Lighting up the world below.

Life below goes endlessly on like life in air,

Swaying rushes, flowers, lilies, standing bent inhaling the soft
breath of nature,
The warm summer breezes, the protecting trees,
Like sentries guarding treasures of the fisher's world.

(Graeme Whiting – 1975)

After moving to Kings Langley I continued to serve as a Territorial
Army (TAVR) officer until 1981, firstly as Training Officer and then
as TAVR Centre Commandant in the 5th Battalion the Royal Anglian
Regiment. This brought my total service tally to eighteen years. In 1980
I became chairman (headteacher) at the Kings Langley school, which
meant that I had to leave the TAVR and resign my commission the
following year. There were strict rules that all TAVR soldiers were obliged
to attend yearly manoeuvres in Germany as a requirement for promotion,
and the school refused to release me.

A year or two before I resigned from the TAVR, we were on our annual
training manoeuvres in Germany, and I found myself in the evenings
sipping sherry in the mess and sharing fishing stories with a helicopter
pilot called Major Alvin Shepherd. He told me a tale about a giant carp
in the old lake at a nearby castle that had been reared almost as a pet by
the Count who owned the place. The major had tried to catch it, but
failed as his equipment was not up to the job. The following week, Al
asked the Count on my behalf if I might try catching this giant, using a
barbless hook so the fish could be returned to the water unharmed.

The Count agreed, and a few days later I went into the castle grounds
after midnight armed with my 11 foot carp rod and a large wooden
frame landing net. There was a lot of loud jollity at the castle, so it was
about 1 a.m. before I started to fish. I was full of adrenaline, with a
degree of trepidation about whether I could land a carp of such immense
proportions and what bait would be best to use. I prepared a 'Whiting
special' of a leathery crust of bread with four large lobworms suspended
beneath it, wound onto a hook with fine silk.

I gently swung the baited line about 10 metres out where it plopped on the surface, making the moon's reflection shimmer in the water. Almost instantly, the lips of a monster carp sucked in the bait and after a few seconds I struck, driving the large hook into its leathery lips. The fight was on; and on and on for more than an hour. Finally, I had the leviathan underneath my rod, which was bent double, and I shone my pin torch into its beautiful eye. Fortunately, at that moment, the castle owner came running along the bank carrying a Hurricane lamp, and between us we managed to lift the creature out of the water and carefully measure and weigh it. The Count actually recognised the fish because of a white spot on its shoulder and he told me he had named her Heidi!

Heidi weighed more than the limit of my 25 kg scales, so the Count ran back to the castle and returned with a set of large old-fashioned weights and scales. We discovered that Heidi weighed a whopping 26.75 kgs or 58 lbs – perhaps the biggest carp in Germany? But in order to protect her from unscrupulous poachers, the Count swore me to secrecy and said we must never disclose Heidi's weight or any details of the catch, except to the few people we could trust. As far as I know, the Count kept the secret until he died in 1982, and I only shared this story with three other anglers, all of whom have now passed away.

I knew it couldn't be registered as my biggest carp, yet I didn't care as I'd landed a real giant. Such a catch caused me to reassess whether it was worthwhile continuing to fish for these magnificent ancient monsters. Was the weight of the fish the most important element of angling, rather than the magic of the fight and the condition of the fish when it was returned to the water? And was big always best?

Meanwhile, at my first Steiner school, with some encouragement and funds from a sponsored walk organised by the students, I dug a big hole in the school grounds, filled it with sand, and created a massive long jump pit. Several children could jump across it at one time, and it became very popular with students in the after-school athletics clubs which often involved over a hundred children.

I was also able to take to the next stage something I'd conceived in 1963 as a young physical training instructor. I loved to perform on the mini trampette, a small, steel-framed device that could whip the gymnast high into the air. When I was performing in the Royal Tournament in 1963 at The Royal Albert Hall, we used inclined ash planks for take-off. Seeing the mini trampette for the first time, I wondered if I could improve it. Perhaps if I welded together two mini trampettes, one in front of the other, and fixed them to the planks so they were rock solid, it would enable a gymnast to safely bounce from the first one onto the second and perform with greater control.

I bought a Mig welder and welded two devices together, reinforcing them with strong wire – the double trampette was born. I took a steady jog towards the new invention and easily managed to spring from the first trampette onto the second. That shot me into the air with such height that I was ready to prove I could not only perform a front somersault, but off my a new invention a double might also be within range; and even maybe a front from the first mini trampette onto the second bed, followed by a double.

Late that evening I prepared the gym and landing area, surrounded the newly created double trampette with floor mats and performed my first double front somersault from this new double act. It seemed fairly easy, and I couldn't wait for the next upper school gym club so I could teach my young gymnasts.

I was privileged to have an overhead rig which meant that I could safely control the students as they learned the more challenging tricks; first a single front somersault and then double fronts – a new challenge for the few who were ready. The landing was superb and controlling each gymnast with this sturdy rig meant there was never an accident.

My ultimate achievement was to do a barani (a straight somersault with a half twist) from the first trampette to land on the second trampette and then go into a double tucked back somersault; all tricks that I'd done many thousands of times.

Within a week I had mastered many new skills that I could teach the students to practise on my new invention. I must have performed at least a hundred barani into double back somersault the following weekend without an accident. At fifteen stones, this was no easy task. I was absolutely elated, and my sleep suffered from hours of designing trick after trick for the children. I worked tirelessly all day plus most evenings and in the holidays to take the physical education programme to its zenith, and we acquired some ace Olympic standard equipment with financial help from the parents. One of our most impressive pieces of kit was 'The Tower', a square, two-storey scaffolding structure that enabled budding gymnasts to jump or somersault off it onto the mats and trampolines below. The students enjoyed apparatus gymnastics enormously, and what they all achieved was staggering.

During physical education lessons and in breaks between lessons, the newly equipped gym became the go-to place for the many children from age six to nineteen who were inspired to learn gymnastics. Every child was welcomed, and no one was ever turned away from our gym clubs. I didn't want any child to ever be treated unkindly with regard to their level of ability. It was my aim, with Sarah's assistance, to make every student feel safe and happy in the gym so they could fully explore the best of what physical education had to offer.

It was a joy to me to see the children gaining in self-confidence, discovering potential they didn't know they had, and developing into stronger, more self-assured young people. This showed me what child-centred education could achieve and helped me to learn more about how I could best teach with kindness and heart, in order to help individual students flourish and realise their capabilities.

Of all the equipment we had, the new double trampette was particularly popular, and I was keen to show it off to one of the Nissan engineers when they came to deliver my new Goliath Trampoline. I showed him the design, giving a fairly good demonstration of a double front somer-sault from the linked devices. He was stunned and impressed, and his smile said it all. This was one of my most exciting inventions!

I performed on my original piece of kit for many years before I was presented with an up-to-date representation of the first commercially created double trampette. This model is still used today, and if I could count how many times I and all the gymnasts I've taught have used a double trampette since I created that first one, it might amount to three million bounces.

My design was a great success, and as I was penniless, it was developed by a company with enough money to make a good job of creating such a valuable piece of gymnastic equipment. Within a few years, the first double trampette, still the current model today, appeared in a catalogue, and I bought two for the school. This elegant device was sensational compared to the first homemade double trampette I'd created with a Mig welder and two planks of wood.


After our long courtship Sarah proposed marriage, and our wedding took place in July 1981 in the Kings Langley church only a stone's throw from the school, with the entire school community invited. It was a large, sumptuous and incredibly joyous occasion, attended by both our families and friends plus all the children we taught, their parents and the school staff. For our honeymoon we spent six weeks travelling round Europe by car, joined at the end by Maxine and Sarah's sister, Charlotte, when we all stayed in the Black Forest with Sarah's old German exchange family. It was a glorious time, and I remember thinking that life couldn't be any better.

When we returned from our honeymoon, Sarah and I lived in the priory adjacent to the school, along with Maxine who was by then a teenager in the upper school. This time we had reasonable accommodation for the three of us plus our dog, Jess, instead of the tiny room in which

Maxine and I had been living. Maxine inherited some funds from her mother and grandmother, and later, after she left school at nineteen, she travelled to Australia, spending time with my brothers, Mick and David, and having adventures working in a variety of jobs.

To add to the good news of my own marriage, my father's life had improved immeasurably after so many years of living unhappily alone, when in 1980 he had married Elsie, the woman who nursed him during the war. He moved to Lincolnshire where they lived contentedly together. He hadn't told his children about the wedding as he knew how much we still loved and missed our mother; but when we found out, we were pleased and relieved to see him finally happy again.

Having always been a workaholic, my father's move to Lincolnshire gave him the impetus to spend more time on his beloved hobbies, especially watch repairing. He also took up gardening and enjoyed writing about his past. Ever willing to learn, he even took driving lessons in his seventies; but he failed his test six times and was told he could drive better in reverse than forwards. The instructor suggested he try flying helicopters!

My dear father had lived such an interesting and active life, but sadly only a year or so after his remarriage he gradually began to grow increasingly frail and incapacitated and was finally diagnosed with terminal lung cancer. His last few weeks were spent in Lincoln General Hospital, where being such a proud man made him a reluctant patient. Unfortunately, while he was in hospital he was cruelly treated by one of the nurses. On my irregular visits I saw my once fit and dapper father, now just skin and bone, lying in a dirty bed in a ward with three other ageing men, clearly all inadequately cared for. By then he could only whisper, and was embarrassed because he wasn't able to speak properly. In his gentle murmurs, I could hear deep sadness and such regret; he realised that a lifetime of smoking had contributed to his illness.

My father whispered that the male nurse who was large and aggressive, was threatening him. Dad told me he was afraid to use a bedpan as the nurse kept swearing at him, and therefore he insisted on struggling, unaided, to get to the bathroom. The other patients confirmed that this nurse had kicked my poor father and then forced him to clean up the faeces leaking out of him as he crawled across the floor on his hands and knees, trying to reach the lavatory.

The three other men told me they experienced the same sort of treatment, but the nurse was a law unto himself and was neither supervised nor managed. These horrendous stories, whispered to me by my dying father, completely broke me. I whispered back that I would make sure the situation was resolved and that he would regain his dignity. When I arranged to meet the hospital administrator he suggested that the nurse was only joking, which made me furious. So I took the necessary action to ensure that justice was done, and the bully was removed.

In 1982, the year after Sarah and I were married, my father died of his lung cancer at the age of seventy-nine. The quality of my father's last days and the manner of his death were extremely distressing to all of his children, and the pain of it has stayed with us.

Although my father was one of six siblings, I didn't know most of my uncles and aunts apart from seeing them at family funerals, since they lived so far away. But I was aware that they were all smokers, as was almost every visitor to our house; sometimes it was a pipe and the pipe smoke choked us all. If only we had known the dangers, but smoking was promoted in the army, air force, and elsewhere, as being a desirable habit. 'Player's Please' was the most common slogan displayed on the huge billboards in our town, followed closely by 'Woodbine – the great little cigarette'. We all smoked from a young age. Why not? It was promoted as being good for one!

In 1984, a couple of years after my father's death, I travelled back to Norfolk with all my flashy, sophisticated carp tackle and bivvy, looking forward to showing off to my old fishing friend and teacher, Triggler

Skoyles. I was sure he would be by the lake, but when I arrived, there was no sign of him. I walked across the fields to his cottage and found his lovely wife, Betty, at home. I asked her where Triggler was and she told me,

'He passed away a few months ago and is in heaven now, probably catching fish. He knew you might call one day so he left you something.'

She handed me a small wooden box and wished me well. The box lid was glued shut so, with tears in my eyes, I put it in my pocket, walked across the fields, collected my gear and drove to my oldest brother Bill's house. When I got there I prised open the lid, and it was full of a fine white powder with a small handwritten note inside saying:

'My fishing friend, a man now. By now you will know that I am happy in heaven catching huge glittering gleaming fish, all day and all night long. I never have to sleep, and I will be by this new-found lake in the sky for a long, long time, hoping that you will use the contents of this box to mix with your bait whenever you fish. I promise, because it is magic dust, you will catch fish as I did, but be sparing as it won't last forever.'

I went home, and every time I fished with paste I mixed in a bit of the white powder and fished with a new confidence, knowing that my friend Triggler had left me his magic powder. I did catch fish, including huge and handsome carp, and always used the powder until a couple of years later when I pushed a piece of bait onto the last remaining powder.

When I visited Norfolk again a few years later, I knocked on Triggler's door, wondering whether his wife would still be there. A rather wrinkly, warm, soft hand vigorously shook mine, gave me a loving embrace and invited me in for a cup of tea – at over ninety-five, Betty was still going strong. She said she knew I would one day want to know the truth about the magic ingredient that I could never bring myself to ask him about.

'Triggler told me before he died, and I want you to know the truth from me, that there was no magic ingredient! Triggler asked me to give you his ashes so that you would scatter them in the water amongst the creatures he loved, the fish he could only imagine but couldn't see, the fish that were beautiful and free. Triggler will be at peace now, and I think he's left his mark on you, has he not?'

Triggler Skoyles was my inspiration and I'm indebted to him for teaching me that the size of a fish is the last thing to worship; that nature, respect and the privilege of being able to fish for these ancient creatures is what leads us to call someone a great fisherman.

# CHAPTER 11

# GLOUCESTERSHIRE

In January 1985, ten years after we'd met and four years after we married, Sarah and I welcomed our first son, William, named after my father and oldest brother.

I'd taught for many years at Kings Langley and had been chairman (headteacher) at the school since 1980. A year after William was born we felt ready for a change. We moved to Gloucestershire where I took a job as a class teacher with a specific interest in physical education in two Rudolf Steiner schools, one after the other. My first post was at Wynstones School near Gloucester, and the second was at a school in Herefordshire. Extraordinarily, this second Steiner school was housed in the same old village school in Much Dewchurch, near Hereford, that my parents had attended as young children.

When I began working at Wynstones in 1986 we bought a house in Leonard Stanley, and I commuted the ten miles to school every day. We lived there for three years, during which time our daughter, Natasha, was born. As well as teaching at Wynstones, I used my personal training and physical education skills to run a small business for a while with Sarah and another couple of people. We started up in 1986 and called the company Threshold Pursuits. Our aim was to introduce young people to a wide variety of outdoor pursuits through a number of nationally recognised centres.

When William was seven, he started school in Class 1 at Wynstones. This was paid for by some kind German Steiner friends of Sarah's, as although I was teaching there, I was not allowed free education for my children. Sadly, due to some bullying, William only lasted a term. He was a keen student who loved school, but the regime could be rather cruel and the bullying wasn't addressed, so he and a few other students left. In contrast, I had an eager and receptive class at the school and enjoyed my teaching role. At the same time, I was pleased to tutor the school's gym teacher, Kim Payne, and train him up to degree level so that he could teach in Australia.

However, the school management was lax with many financial irregularities, so I only stayed for two years and then left. During my time at Wynstones I became College Chairman (headteacher), but I had no real say in the management, and I didn't feel that the school was sufficiently committed to Steiner's ideals. My experience at this school taught me a lot about leadership and how a flawed system could fail to honour the children who were meant to be its prime concern. I tried hard to rid the school of negative issues, which made me unpopular as I had to confront those who I felt were out of order. But the number and gravity of unaddressed problems between the different factions at the school soon led me to move to the school in Hereford.

Some years previously my sister, Joan, and I had gone to look around Bodenham, the village where she and most of our siblings were born. Joan wanted to visit Much Dewchurch, and we looked inside the Steiner school where the school's founder and her husband were fitting a reinforced steel joist into the floor of a newly created classroom on the first floor. We chatted with them, and in jest, the founder suggested that maybe one day I would teach at the school. Fulfilling the prophecy, I became a teacher there in 1988 – with my parents' childhood classroom eventually becoming my own classroom in 1991.

At the time I started teaching in Hereford Maxine was still living and travelling in Australia, and we had William and Natasha at home, both under four. After a year we moved to a lovely fourteenth century black-and-white cottage called 'The Butts' at Brockworth, which made life easier as it was closer to Hereford. We were incredibly happy there and spent much of our spare time doing it up, feeling rather like a team of professional painters and decorators. Sarah also enjoyed her own creative painting, making the children's clothes, writing stories and poems and engaging in a variety of art and crafts. She was always busy ensuring that William and Natasha were very well looked after in a comfortable home. Going off to teach every day, I was in awe of my wife's good nature and abundant creative, home building and childcare skills.

As my pay was so low, Sarah took in washing and ironing and cleaned people's houses in order to make enough money to send the children to kindergarten. These were challenging times, especially for Sarah, as we were still improving the house, and she was engaged in her own creative activities plus working and caring for our home and young children and our faithful black Labrador, another Jasper. When I arrived back from Hereford on my motorbike at five in the afternoon, I was able to take charge of the children which was a pleasure, especially as it meant I could offer my wife a break.

I enjoyed teaching my class at the Hereford school, but partially echoing the situation at Wynstones, the way the school was being run left a lot to be desired. I was Chairman of the College of Teachers (headteacher) and so it was incumbent upon me to look back at situations that had taken place before my time, including some very serious issues involving abuse that in today's world would have prompted legal action. A few of the teachers were out of their depth and were not really Steiner inspired. Some of the parents had a rather mercurial disposition, and a number were quite rebellious and defiant, so it was difficult to keep our interactions calm and sensible. Communication was not straightforward, and there was much dishonesty and denigratory talk behind people's backs.

A small group of parents met with me in private and said that if I wanted to take over the school and oust the founders, they would stand with me because they felt that these founders were holding the school back and preventing change. It was difficult for me to hear this and to contemplate being disloyal to those colleagues whom I respected; and it didn't feel right to act at that time. So in July 1990 I gave a year's notice, during which time I heard that different factions of teachers and parents were vying with each other and plotting to take over the leadership of the school, eager to see me gone as soon as possible. As always, of course, it is the children who suffer most in these fraught situations.

During this period, in the summer of 1990, Sarah and I had a distressing experience that delivered a harsh blow. Our home was robbed, and we lost almost everything of value. Expensive and prized original paintings that were gifts to our children from their grandfather, a stereo, the jewellery I'd bought for Sarah, a nineteenth century grandfather clock made from walnut which was one of Sarah's heirlooms, and even our washing machine, were all stolen. We were fairly sure who the burglar was but could do nothing about it under the current legal system and weren't able to recover any of the stolen items. As a small recompense for our loss, the insurance payout was helpful later on, when we used it to keep my own new school afloat for a while.

My very low salary meant that while I was still teaching at Hereford, I had to take second and third jobs in order to support our growing family – our second son, James, was born in September 1990. I worked in London as a swimming coach in an exclusive swim school, travelling 200 miles by motorcycle on a Saturday, having left home at four o'clock in the morning and ridden back with chlorine-filled eyes in the evening. I was utterly exhausted as I had spent five hours on the motorbike and taught swimming for six hours non-stop to more than seventy children.

By the summer of 1991, my last year at Hereford, I calculated I had ridden 80,000 miles on my motorbike, worn out eight sets of tyres, spent over £1,500 on servicing and approximately £3,000 on petrol! That took up much of the salary I was drawing at the time. I had a mortgage, insurances, needed food to eat, and with the rest of my earnings had to clothe us all. These were hard times indeed. The teachers at that school once told a friend of mine that I was being overpaid and should be ashamed of drawing such a large salary, which was apparently the highest in Steiner education at that time. Utter poppycock!

I remember that at one time when we ran out of money, we were living off army rations I'd kept from my time in the army. The bully beef, suet pudding, baked beans and hardtack (army biscuits) seemed to make quite a nutritious meal in those difficult times.

With all my jobs, there was just enough to keep our family afloat, but there was nothing left for a holiday or any extras. We all benefited from the children's camps in Devon that I organised for several years and that later had to suffice as holidays for our children. Every year I took about thirty young teenagers on these adventure holidays, which was enormous fun. In the early years before our children were old enough to come on the camps, Sarah would stand in the corner of a field holding the hands of William and Natasha, with baby James in her arms, waving goodbye to me each day as I drove off with the various groups. Happily, from 1992 as the children grew, Sarah was able to bring them on the camps. Little did I know back in those early days that I would have five children who were all really active and shared my enthusiasm for adventure.

Transport was tricky at that time, and cars always induce a sense of unease in me – maybe because I love them so much. While I was conceiving my own school idea, I owned a rickety old Ford, not fit for purpose and which was in need of constant repairs; whenever it broke down, I had to find a way of earning the extra money to fix it. In 1990 I owned a Volvo, worth about £800, which I gave to my close friends, Nick and Marion, as a gift. People never cease to amaze me, and those two wonderful people, the salt of the earth, gave me the entire proceeds when they eventually sold the car. They never knew how much their generosity saved us from the courts, since through no fault of our own we had been blacklisted with a County Court Judgment for not being able to honour our debts.

Throughout these difficult times I was always imagining what kind of school I might create – and there was no doubting that it would be a mighty challenge.

From all my different teaching activities I had learned a great deal about children of all ages, but I was aware that I was surrounded by teams of teachers who really knew very little about the deeper aspects of human development and who were content to use rigid old-fashioned attitudes to learning that couldn't really achieve the high quality of education that I was seeking and longing to create. It was all too rigorously state examination orientated, and the routes for students towards an adult life and a meaningful profession were very cluttered.

There is a thick mist or fog around potential career paths for young people in this country. When I was at school, we were all pushed towards specific jobs without really understanding what they were about, so most of us entered adult life and employment without really having a clue. I was once recommended to become a chicken sexer at Birds Eye!

By the late 1980s I was seriously reassessing my life and career to date and feeling the need to find a new path – a way forward that was satisfying. I could see it would certainly not be as an employee, as I had opposing views to those of my peers and employers. I knew that I could only realise my ideals if I had my own school. I needed to create something of my own through my own initiative; a school that manifested my educational vision and where standards were high. I needed to build my own golden chalice! I had qualified as a physical training teacher in 1964, so by the end of the eighties I'd been teaching soldiers and children for twenty-six years and was forty-six years old.

# CHAPTER 12

# FOUNDING ACORN

When I gave a year's notice in 1990 and resigned from the school in Hereford, I was determined to start my own school, and as my teaching there came to a close, I intended to let destiny take a hand. At that time, starting a new school was just about impossible, and with minus £38 in the bank, how would I do it? Nevertheless, I took the step, ably aided by Sarah. Together we would sacrifice everything for our dream of creating a school of outstanding quality; and it would also ensure we could teach our own children.

In contemplating the next phase, I'd been looking forward to being able to muster the courage to take this massive stride. But what was motivating me in that direction?

My ambition was to create an exemplary school in which young people would be treated with kindness so that they could learn and grow up to fully understand the world in which they live. This would encourage them to be compassionate and helpful, to uphold the right of every human being to be who they have chosen to be, and to never look down on or criticise those who may be less privileged and may have chosen a different path from that which is considered traditional and normal. During the years I taught in Steiner schools, I was tremendously inspired by Rudolph Steiner's philosophy of education. In order to achieve the standard of education I envisaged, I was moved to update the Steiner system to be as beneficial now as it was in its early days.

My vision resonated closely with Rudolf Steiner's words:

'It is not wars that change the world. It is not power that changes the world. It is not money that changes the world. It is individuals who follow their inner spark, called potential, who need to be encouraged through a holistic education, despite the walls that are put before them, to follow their potential to become uniquely confident and free-thinking adults.'

I discovered that Steiner touches on the golden chalice in his meditations. By this time the chalice had come to symbolise for me the unique, loving heart of life, shining in each human being, as well as the school that can nurture and foster this attribute. My wife, my children, my school vision and my view of the core of humanity, especially in children, all seemed to have the essence of purity that to me is embodied in the image of the golden chalice.

We tend to look for the faults in people instead of embracing their higher self. But inside every new-born child is the potential to become a great human being. This potential can either be encouraged or quashed by the education system. Looking back over my life, and in particular at those parts that required study – my school days, gaining a fine art diploma part time in two years and training for a teaching diploma in the army – I am aware that there were many periods when I met the opposite of what I consider education should be.

When I was a child there was poverty in my education as well as in my home. I was often bored at school and relatively unstimulated by all but one teacher, my junior school teacher, Major Charlie Philips. Through his leadership and strength he taught me how to value my individuality and creativity and to develop the confidence to rise above adversity, negativity, criticism and persecution. Through his wisdom and care for the children he taught, I learned so many important and helpful life lessons.

Now I found myself standing on the edge of an unknown abyss and envisaging the struggle I might take on through the force of my own strength of will and determination, in order to create an exceptional school that would manifest those values. I realised it would be tough, but I was undaunted as I had Sarah by my side, and with her support and commitment, I knew that together we could go through anything – and we have!

Over seven million children attend school in this country, and they have one thing in common: they are all unique individuals, different human beings who are immersed in outdated systems that treat each child as a member of the group dynamic in a class of similar-aged children. This is how education is delivered today – not to each individual but to a group.

This is a flawed and unkind educational concept, unless the class is small enough and the teacher sufficiently capable of properly and holistically educating each individual child. My vision is that children can be seen as the unique individuals they are and receive an education of substance, studying those subjects that will be invaluable in this fast-changing world.

I rue the day government education gurus decided that bigger is better. Look back at the village schools in the pre-WWII period and see what they produced in the way of eminent and successful people; a system copied from the late nineteenth century.

In the 1950s, despite its often strict and harsh application, British education was considered the best in the world. In my younger days in the early sixties, when I sped across the south of England to attend lectures by outstanding professors in medical science and related psychology, I was an eager learner with a sharp memory. I seem to have retained much of what I was taught by those excellent teachers, and can still recall many academic facts that became a feature of my later teaching life.

But after the government got its hands on education during the sixties and played around at the behest of so-called educational experts arguing in 'alternative thinking' groups, we saw a rapid, and in my opinion incalculable, decline in education. Government after government tweaked it, and individuals who knew little about child development tampered with its tenets in order to encourage education to motivate and force children to compete child against child, with the ones who were able to answer the set questions creamed off to so-called outstanding universities. What, for instance, about those young people who are late developers?

In schools and universities there used to be opportunities for inspiring teaching, but in the existing world a lot of youngsters don't love learning as I used to, neither at school nor in university; maybe partly because life has become so cyber-ridden. It seems that the tickets called university degrees are more important than the process of learning, even though very few young graduates use their degrees after university.

It would be wonderful if university education could be revamped and updated, so that every young person was given the right to take whatever path they chose, without labels, and within an upgraded and human-centred system of higher education that genuinely encouraged everyone's true potential. This would mean a complete reorganisation of the teaching system, of teacher training colleges, and of our understanding of our world, so that individuality would be treasured, and young people would be given the right to be who they wish to be through a well-designed educational system created by people who truly understood. However, the trend seems to be currently heading in the opposite direction, towards universities operating as businesses whose main purpose is to groom their customers (students) for the narrow requirements of the employment market.

Today's education system is the result of several decades of misman-agement, largely at the hands of career politicians, many of whom had a public-school education and who constantly criticise each other. There is an attendant disregard for the collateral damage being done to children, often from the wrong decisions made as a consequence of a lack of intelligence and understanding of people's true needs. British education is not the cutting-edge world-beating system that is often being lauded on television by whoever happens to be the Education Secretary; but it was and it could be again!

Wisdom often seems to lie outside government, and our fast-changing governments have made many avoidable mistakes to the detriment of society; for example, the strongly recommended sixties high-rise blocks which can trap families in their cell-like homes, especially when public spaces may be out of bounds, for example during a pandemic. Alongside all the major errors, we must of course honour and pay tribute to the many exceptional and positive changes in society that have made the world a much more equal and agreeable place in which to live; but I wouldn't include the realm of education in that category.

I wanted to create a school which showed that young people can be taught to a very high academic level without using the models of state or public school education, both of which in my opinion have failed to broadly educate. Education is not about testing.

After much contemplation, I knew it was finally time to start my own school – the school I dreamt of creating all that time ago in the school hall where I was whacked across the arse by Mr Wilkins.

Ironically, although I rejected the cruelty and brutality of those early years, I incorporated into my own school a lot of basic principles from my childhood education such as: form, order, manners, attentive listening, and a very high standard of physical education. What I did veto was any form of detention or punishment, as that only alienates the child from the teacher. I am against persecution, judgment or labelling, preferring to work with individual children to help them navigate their natural developmental stages at their own pace. Many schools focus almost solely on team sports like football, to the detriment of gymnastics and individual sports; but I was determined to give every child the right to access a wide range of physical activities.

In the army I learned to lead by example and discovered that by doing this, you don't need to punish people for not coming up to your high standards. So from the army I brought to my own school the adage of Exemplo Ducemus: By Example Shall We Lead. I encouraged my students to embrace some of the qualities that the army taught me – smartness, cleanliness, self-respect, and respect for older people who possess the wisdom of their experience. I also endorsed the principle of Virtute et Veritate: With Courage and Truth; especially the importance of finding in oneself the willingness and courage to face adversity.

In 1991 I founded and created The Acorn School which is now based in Nailsworth, Gloucestershire. On 16 September 1991, the very first day of my new school, the initial four children were welcomed, and we effectively had a school, albeit with only a few children. We had one classroom – a rather rough conservatory at our home, The Butts, in Brockworth, which offered a space of seventy square feet, a table, five chairs and some paper and wax blocks.

The children were so happy, and they smiled throughout the first part of the main lesson. To them it was a real adventure, as it was for me and Sarah. Joby had followed me from Hereford and was the founding pupil; Shanti and Kunsang came from a nearby independent kindergarten, and Rammiel came from the local area. None had money for fees, except the founding child whose father was an osteopath, but I nevertheless enthusiastically taught these delightful children whose parents had taken 'the road less travelled'.

At 11 a.m. on the first morning, I filled my car with the four children and drove to Cooper's Hill, near Painswick. Cooper's Hill, known as the cheese rollers' hill, is where we used to take our children to see the gnomes' houses and the gently swaying trees. Ash, beech, maple, sycamore and one huge acorn-laden oak tree all stand amidst the acres of wild garlic which are hidden under the mossy ground in autumn. The air was filled with the sweet smells of nature.

When we sat on top of the hill, looking across to the west and eating our snacks, a walker passed by. He looked at me and the children and asked us who and what we were. Joby, full of innocent glee, said,

'We are the smallest school in the world.'

When the man had continued on his way, the children told me they didn't want any more children to join the school; how cool was that?

I was overjoyed – here were four satisfied children at a new school, my school, a school with no building other than a hill on which to sit in the midst of the glorious Cotswold countryside, looking west to where the Roman legions had marched in the fifth century; what an image.

By the end of the week there were three more children, and on the following Monday 23 September we moved the school to Edge Farm where Shanti and Kunsang lived. Their home had a large and stunningly attractive refectory which was offered to us by their parents in lieu of fees. It was a magnificent place to teach; a long room with a handsome centuries-old oak table round which I sat with all seven pupils.

The children had come from schools where they weren't happy and were not really seen as individuals. I saw them as delightful young people, true individuals, seemingly happy and contented after only a week at their new school. All were from somewhat alternative families whose parents had found the courage to walk a different path.

There in that room, my new schoolroom, I started to teach the curriculum I had written. I arrived an hour and a half before school started every morning after driving my old car half an hour through breathtakingly beautiful Cotswold countryside. Over the next few weeks we continued to grow rapidly. Not many schools double in size during one week!

At the beginning of the second week, the small group of children were already arriving each morning an hour before school started. When I arrived I lit an open fire with wood I'd found under some nearby trees, which warmed and lit up the refectory. I was soon playing my guitar and singing to the children as they gazed into the flickering autumn firelight, hurrying to take their places at the huge table. One child saw salamanders dancing in the flames. They were all smiling, though there was one smile standing out amongst the group: mine!

It was magical, but the peace was soon disturbed on day three of the second week of our new school by the arrival of a large black car. The car pulled up ever so quietly outside. Someone had a large spoon and could stir the pot very effectively – it was clear that the school from whence three of the children had come had called the local education department to report me.

Oh dear! Did the people who made that call think that I could summarily be shut down? Did they ever consider that the children who had left their previous school were withdrawn because the education it offered wasn't working for them?

I sat at the head of the table surrounded by these lovely, smart, happy young children with eyes wide open waiting to be taught, and a strong and determined group of happy parents too. Alfred Lord Tennyson's 'The Charge of the Light Brigade' came to mind: 'Into the school of light strode the few children.' What could spoil such a remarkable little school where the pupils were contented and fulfilled?

Two people wearing black coats alighted from the car, gently shut the car doors and knocked on the school door with its huge lion's head knocker. I opened the door and welcomed them into the schoolroom. These uninvited guests were happy to join in the song we were singing, 'Leaving on a Jet Plane'. But after the last verse had finished they informed me that they were the local Educational Authority representatives who had heard there was a school here which had no permission.

When I asked them how they knew I had started a school when it was so hidden by a forest, they freely gave the name of the person, one of my ex-colleagues, who had reported me. I assured them that we were going to apply for permission, and as they left they clearly seemed taken with what I was doing and said that the atmosphere was truly wonderful.

That first term at the farm was joyous. I was lucky to be joined by my first teacher, Lucy, a highly intelligent and gifted young teacher. She sang along with me every morning with her heavenly voice. One day Lucy and I were walking with the children on Selsley Common when we saw some large white stones over on the hillside. The children began playing with the stones and trying to make letters, starting with A. Since they were so young, they were having a bit of trouble with the letter B so they moved on to something easier, a circle as in the letter C. Then Lucy said,

'Why don't you write ACORN? We could call it The Acorn School.'

And The Acorn School was named!

Sarah offered to become the bursar of our new school. She was guided by the school's accountant and proved to be an excellent bursar and record keeper. Sarah and I handmade all the children's schoolbooks whilst at home in the evenings when our children were asleep. I can see my loyal wife now, sitting by the fire in our living room in Brockworth, happily humming while she worked. I was thrilled by her support, and it reminded me of the famous words from William Blake as he sat sewing his books with his wife, Kate:

'Stay. You have ever been an angel to me. I will draw you!'

By the end of that initial term six new children had registered, and we needed more space. So we left the farm in January 1992 and moved the school into an old school building in Stroud called The British School, where I rented a large hall with many stringent and absurd conditions. I wondered whether the government officials would be tipped off about our move, but they were preempted, as Acorn's new home was an established school building with planning permission.

The new hall was certainly large enough, though very expensive to rent, and there were many daily, often spontaneously contrived conditions, such as packing away every trace of the school each afternoon so that nobody renting the hall after school time could see there was a school there. We were allowed no entry after school hours and specifically no singing loudly enough to be heard by the people earning their living in the offices surrounding the school hall. I think this condition was forced upon me because some of the children had left a nearby school to come to Acorn, and those departures had caused a few sour grapes. Some parents of that school had their businesses in the building, and I suspected that the people who owned the building tried to make sure I couldn't continue to function there long-term, hence also the concocted rent rises.

The numerous walls that were erected during my time renting The British School in Stroud, many fabricated instantaneously to try and close down our new school, seemed to be built in the most extraordinary places and were thicker than the city wall built a thousand years ago around Gloucester!

Stroud is a small Cotswold town lying in a most scenic natural area amidst rolling hills with views across the west towards the River Severn and Wales. I didn't especially choose to move the school to Stroud; it was a matter of Hobson's choice and Stroud chose Acorn. But at that time Stroud was a rather hostile place to have a small independent school.

So in September 1992, after a large number of new children applying and a huge rent increase clearly designed to get me out, I moved Acorn to a Georgian mansion in the village of Thrupp, a mile outside Stroud, where we were given a flat for our family plus enough rooms for the school. Sarah and I were sad to be selling our family home at The Butts, where William, Natasha and James had been so happy, but glad to have a place to live in such a beautiful setting alongside Acorn where William had already started in Class 1. During this time Maxine was living in Bristol and working at selling advertising for a magazine. She was in constant contact with us and was very proud of our little school.

The owner was fine about having a school on the premises, and an Acorn parent, Sandra Bruce, already lived there so she effectively arranged for the move from Stroud. Sandra will always be 'an Acorn angel'. She single-handedly saved my school, and I will forever be indebted to her and her daughter, Hannah, who attended Acorn from when she was six.

Acorn's fourth home within a year was set in the midst of the Cotswold hills at Thrupp, on a lovely site with grounds of about an acre, an old coaching house, some stables, a tennis court, and a magnificent large Georgian building. A mulberry tree graced one area of the grounds and was visible to the children from their classrooms; with the added bonus of a crop of extraordinarily large mulberries at the end of summer. There was a big maple tree for the children to play under during breaks. We even set up a trampoline on the tennis court for when the weather permitted its use during breaks and gym lessons. The whole place was delightful and the rooms we used for lessons had old-fashioned corniced ceilings and were perfect for education.

Our classrooms and my family's living accommodation were both hurriedly painted by those willing parents who continually gave so much time to the Acorn vision; though we weren't ready to move into our flat until after the first term. They were an extraordinary team of caring and enthusiastic people who worked diligently to help us create a bona fide school building. It was uplifting and encouraging to be given such support, and although many people helped, Janette and Stephen Hall stand out as the most committed and kind school parents one could ever find. Their unstinting and continual backing was one element that helped give me the confidence I needed to jump over those high walls. I owe these two magnificent people so very much. They even left bread and other items of food outside our door as a token of support, and that gesture reminded me of the loaves and fishes; my family of five could be fed.

On one occasion, Janette, who later became an Acorn teacher, was working away from the town, and she slipped her weekly wage packet through my letterbox as she went home after a long day working in a café. She had left the pay slip inside, and when I opened the envelope, I saw that she had not taken a penny. I think this might be the most moving gift I've ever received from a parent, and it was received with the same love with which it was given.

To our utter shock and disbelief, after only one term at The Thrupp, the authorities wanted us closed down and wrote to me giving notice to move. Of course, we had no other premises to where we could relocate the school. Apparently, the giant old ash tree that stood proudly about ten feet from one of the gate pillars at the entrance to the school drive, had four huge roots and one of them was growing across the drive, hardly rising more than half an inch above the ground. It was, as the local council's representative who visited told me, obstructing the passage of parents' cars in and out of the drive. This was enough to deny any application to continue there as a registered school and was clearly an invented excuse. I engaged 'The Men of the Trees', a strong and knowledgeable oak-like group of tree experts who came to examine the ash tree and give their opinion:

'I think that such a tree could easily manage with even two roots,' said the main man, and I thanked them for their wisdom.

The numerous other people who visited the ash tree were also clear that Stroud Town Council were just finding an excuse to move us out. Many people came from the area to look at the root and some even knocked at the school door and asked where it was. The local news reporters were very interested in this root, and one asked to attend school for a morning. She was a retired headteacher, and she sat in my classroom at the end of the morning with tears in her eyes, visibly distressed at what was happening.

The county educational authority paid many visits whilst the school was functioning and were clearly impressed. But they had strong views about independent education, which showed in a letter I received on 24 November, stating that because of the tree root, no permission could be given for the school to continue, not even if parents dropped their children off at the gate or even at the bottom of the hill on the busy A46. We needed a helicopter!

The following morning as I walked down the drive to the school gates, I noticed to my amazement that there was no longer a root across the drive, nor was there any sign that there had ever been one. Strange, I thought – someone must have come along in the night and chopped off this vital root. Jumping ahead, I can report that the ash tree is still thriving in 2022 – without its infamous root.

We were forced to pack up the school again and say goodbye to those splendid grounds, thanking and honouring that space, a place we had occupied for only ninety days. Did we really build a school in that time and leave with almost thirty pupils? By the end of the Michaelmas Term 1992 the school had tripled, reminding me of an old proverb that seemed apt for both the school and my new life as its founder and headteacher: 'Great oaks from little acorns grow.'

At the final assembly carol concert, I made an announcement that the school would not be occupying The Thrupp next term, that the Council had refused to accept our operating there because of the tree root issue, and that I had no other building. One parent stood up and declared on behalf of all but one of them, that they would wait for me to contact them after Christmas to tell them where to bring the children next term – a field or any space at all would be fine, just let them know! I was humbled.

Then on the last day of term, we were blessed to receive a telephone call from a parent who informed us that a state school was closing down in Nailsworth on that very day, and they wondered whether we were interested. Yes we were, and we were suddenly elated! For this, I will be eternally grateful to Richard Valentine.

After school on that final day of our only term at The Thrupp, Sarah and I hurried to Nailsworth, with William, Natasha and James in the back of our old car, to view this as yet unseen Church school building which was closed up with huge sheets of softwood nailed over the windows. We arrived just as the last nail was being driven into the window frames. How could we get this ready-to-use school building? Where could I find a home for my family, and how could I pay the rent?

Our first task was to hire the school building as we had no money to buy it, but this proved to be extremely difficult. The Church owned it and it was let out by a notable local land agent who wanted £25,000 p.a. rent for this tired boarded-up and disgracefully presented now ex-state school.

The building had been a girls' public school in the 1830s and since then many other schools had been in occupation. To ask the agents to rent a Church school building to a man who wanted to set up an independent school seemed an impossibility. Nevertheless, after a considerable amount of haggling and stress, I managed to rent it and Acorn moved in.

Now was the start of many periods of rental accommodation, of state support, of little food and the potential of a derelict and tired school building to restore. I looked at Sarah and as always, she embraced me and said that we should think positively; and so long as we had each other, our lovely children and a vision, all would work out. Just stand strong, she insisted.

# CHAPTER 13

# THE ACORN SCHOOL: MY GOLDEN CHALICE

On 9 January 1993 I received the keys to our excellent, though partly derelict, school building in Nailsworth. We were in the midst of huge upheaval since we were in the process of moving our family into the rented flat back at The Thrupp, having just sold our home in Brockworth. But at supper that night I was overcome with joy and relief. After the places Acorn had previously occupied, this was a palace, a generic Victorian school building that had everything necessary for education. My golden chalice finally had a home.

The building had been left in a very sorry state by its previous incumbents, the local primary school. The winter weather outside was warmer than the temperature in the school hall when I first opened the door and walked in holding a fluttering candle in a jam-jar, my hand shaking with excitement and anticipation.

I set about taking down the boarding and tackling the other jobs on my own. It took three days in temperatures of about minus five degrees to draw out more than five thousand nails and picture pins, using an ancient borrowed claw hammer and with blood oozing from one of my fingers. Several hundredweight of boards were removed from the beautiful windows and doors and then piled up ready to be discarded.

Within a couple of days, the heating pipes throughout the school began to thaw, and it was clear that most were broken, so we had to deal with floods from burst pipes before we could open for business. With no money, I set about repairing and replacing where needed, which took several days.

The hall floor was rotting and was probably the original; it was damp, well used and rather scruffy. I walked towards the edge to check the state of the floor timber and fell through a rotten section of flooring. I wondered how it was possible for the state to care so little about such a lovely structure. The electrics were poor, the heating system was broken, there were gas leaks, and the toilets were grim. It was just a freezing cold, scruffy old school building, but I was overjoyed. I had to be – it was all we had!

Our first week went well, although after school each day I had to hand the keys over to the agents as we were not allowed in the building after four o'clock and certainly not at weekends. To have tried to push things might have meant us losing the lease, so we were very much at the mercy of the Church and their unhelpful, unfriendly estate agents. These agents were absolutely useless, refused to fix anything and didn't care a jot. And nor did The Diocese of Gloucester, the owners of the site, just as long as we paid the rent. There was some legal requirement to help us, but the Church did nothing, just as the agents did nothing but collect the hard-earned rent; and I couldn't push it in case we were evicted. I soon realised that, at some point, we would need to buy it.

A local Church of England Canon from Minchinhampton, the nearest town, came and saw the building we were renting and was appalled. There was absolutely no effort to help us, and I was told that before we moved in, the school building had been declared on the verge of being derelict and effectively unfit for education. Where was the heart in the Church of England? The Canon made some protestations to The Bishop, but to no avail, so we had no choice other than to soldier on and make sure we could pay the staff and honour the rent. Where was God in all this, I wondered?

Although there was much excitement, it was clear to the parents that there was still a great deal to do and that we would get no help from the agents or the Church. During the first year of our renovations Sarah was off limits for much of the time as far as manual labour was concerned as she was at that time pregnant with our youngest son, Oliver, who was born the following year in 1994. But we had a school building, a curriculum, a full staff of teachers and the required stationery. With the school building secured, it was appropriate to ensure that the curriculum I wrote in the first year of Acorn was updated and amended so we could move forwards. Ofsted were looking now.

After my earlier years in three Steiner schools as chairman (headteacher), class teacher and specialist teacher, I fully endorse the phenomenal quality of the curriculum created by Steiner. I have nothing but support for any Steiner educational initiatives, provided they are started with wisdom and a true understanding of the finer elements of Steiner education. I profoundly support pure Steiner education, though not in the way that it is often manifested, and it is sad that many Steiner schools have been closed. I could not name any current Steiner school in this country as being a true replica of what Steiner suggested or would even countenance today if he were alive.

In Acorn, we have practised and upheld much of Rudolph Steiner's Lower school curriculum, but I created my own Upper school curriculum which we have been using extremely successfully for thirty years. Our school curriculum is accepted by Ofsted, even though it could be considered to be the antithesis of government education.

Anthroposophy, on the other hand, is a path of knowledge and a personal philosophy specifically for those people who choose to follow it, and it has no place in education. Any attempt to indoctrinate children into that pathway is inappropriate as it is a purely personal study and should not be part of education.

Physical education has always been one of the keystones of education at Acorn, with the aim of improving all aspects of the children's health and enhancing their physical capabilities and self-confidence. So as soon as we had suitable premises I was eager to start putting to use all my experience of gymnastics and gym inventions since 1975, in order to give the children a top-class gym. At Dean Close and Kings Langley I'd had excellent fully-equipped gyms and sports facilities, but here I had to pretty much start from scratch. My first step was to relive my high horse vaulting past and bring that to the school's physical education programme. I asked a skilled craftsman, Stephen Hall, to create a supremely functional high horse for vaulting, with telescopic legs and the capacity to be raised from six to nine feet in a few minutes. The remaining issue was that I needed a soft padded leather top, so it was safe for the children to vault over.

I took some of my students to the Jaguar factory, and after being shown around we arrived at the area where the famous Jaguar seats were covered in high quality cowhide. Aha, I saw what I wanted – a huge skin for the top of my horse. I appealed to the boss, and a visit was arranged to the school to see what would work. A month later two men in dark suits arrived at the school in a sleek Jaguar, gliding gently into the front car park. The children's faces were pressed against the classroom windows in wonder.

After a quick look at Stephen's topless high horse, the men announced that they couldn't give me a cowhide. I was disappointed, and after my pleading, one of the men suggested that perhaps it might be acceptable if they took the dimensions and created a wooden detachable top, covered in a hide on top of a layer of thick sponge.

'Give me the top and I will take it back to my boss and see what we can do, but I make no promises.'

His expression, though, made all the promises I needed.

A month later it arrived, along with the same men in a Ford Transit with the name 'Jaguar' emblazoned on the side. Children and teachers poured out of the school entrance into the car park with a degree of animation I have rarely seen; the excitement was tangible, particularly from me!

The joy was phenomenal and yet not one student had ever seen a high horse. The newly made top fitted perfectly and this high horse is still in the school's gym hall where it stands proudly as an example of innovation and support from Jaguar Cars and fine skill from Stephen Hall.

I estimate that in the last thirty years, over three million hands have touched the leather top whilst vaulting, and it is still in perfect condition with little sign of wear. Thank you to Jaguar Cars; that year I changed my car to a Jaguar!

Before the end of 1992, I had equipped the hall with two Olympic-sized trampolines, two double trampettes, a couple of single trampettes, parallel bars, an Olympic beam, Reuter board, pommel horse, three vaulting horses, enough gym mats to cover the floor, and an overhead rig for teaching double somersaults.

The early staff who joined me in our first year at Nailsworth were a stellar group of talented people, and all were dedicated to my ideals. Throughout my time as Acorn headteacher, I trained all the teachers who came to the school, irrespective of their formal qualifications, because my educational vision was different from what most of them had encountered before. As was to be expected, the transition from one form of education to a new one was difficult for some teachers, particularly for a few who had previously been in the Steiner system. All new teachers were required to attend training for one evening a week over two years, so that they could be thoroughly imbued with my system and the school's ethos. It was a pleasure to teach them, as they were invariably won over by the intelligence and kindness of Acorn education.

In 1994 we were briefly joined by my friend and former Dean Close pupil, Jeremy Wade, who worked at Acorn as a biology teacher for six months. He was an extremely popular teacher, also teaching basic Italian to the upper school and then accompanying us on one of our school trips to France and Italy. It was a joy to have Jeremy's talents and extraordinary intellect with us at the school for a while.

While we were working to establish and upgrade the school, the Church of England and the Diocese of Gloucester continued doing many things to stop us succeeding. They were antagonistic towards me and the children, probably because it was an independent school. There was a rule preventing us from even entering the church, which was adjacent to the school building, and the vicar was openly hostile. My grandfather was a C. of E. vicar in 1860, and the kind of image the current diocese presented to me was shocking and far removed from what William Thomas Whiting endorsed. Had he been alive, I'm sure he would have armed himself with some choice words of wisdom for the bishop!

With a huge amount of hard work and a lot of help from friends, in the winter of 1995, two years after we'd moved in, we were finally able to buy the school buildings and the entire near-derelict site from the Church; it was now ours. On the day we confirmed the purchase, Sarah and I drove to Gloucester with our young children in a broken-down car with a flat battery and no money, not even enough to scrape a supper. But we did it, we jolly well did it! Nothing could stand in our way now, not even the Church.

The purchase of the building was a huge step in the security of the school, and I am greatly indebted to my friend and class teacher, Richard Valentine, now sadly deceased, who was instrumental in securing a mortgage so that we could buy the school site. I am also incredibly grateful to Vicky and Alan Macdonald and family, to one of the children's grandparents, to Terry Oldfield, to John and Linda Meletiou and to

Janette and Stephen Hall, who between them loaned us enough to pay the required deposit. All now life-long friends and Honourable Friends of The Acorn School. I was jubilant on the day we were able to pay them all back with interest.

An Acorn benefactor, my dear friend, Terry Oldfield, was one of the shining stars in my life in those days and always held my hand through the dark times of having no money. I taught his eldest daughter, Rachel, at Wynstones School and thereafter all his children were educated at Acorn. Sarah was beside me and not only encouraged me with each step, but also worked tirelessly to help to establish the school. I owe Acorn to her, for no other wife could ever have been so devoted to her husband's educational philosophy, while having to live in such poverty, with the family all wearing secondhand clothes, and at times enduring a subsistence diet of bread and jam or army tack and compo rations (tinned and packaged food for soldiers).

In the early years of Acorn, Sarah was mostly engaged in looking after our four youngest children, William, Natasha, James and Oliver, as well as making the main lesson and subject lesson books and supporting my commitment to outdoor education, especially the school trips. Each school book was carefully made, hand sewn with needle and string and neatly trimmed with a craft knife. The countless hours we spent and the hard work we put in are almost unimaginable when I think about it now. It came from our commitment to the children, and we did it joyfully and with dedication to the pupils who would value our creations. We were unequivocally committed to the school and to having the very best we could provide at the time. But the materials were the least important element in these early days; we finally had a real school building, and we loved it.

At the time we bought the school, our own children were aged ten, eight, three and one. They were happy to stay in the school with us each day after lessons and help us, mostly playing on the mats and having fun while Sarah and I, as proud new owners, painted, swept, polished, cleaned and generally upgraded our Acorn home.

Sarah and I were on the same page regarding raising our children, and we adopted much of the wisdom of Rudolf Steiner's guidelines in parenting. In essence, we saw our children as unique individuals, allowing each of them to develop at their own pace, loving them and ensuring they were brought up with care and respect for their sensitivities, with no punishments, shouting or chastisements. We put our children to bed early each evening, and after bathtime Sarah and I would read them stories together, over and over again. Sometimes William, nine years older than Oliver, along with Natasha and James, would all be lying on the bed next to me and Sarah, reading to Oliver. This nightly ritual greatly strengthened our vision of parenting and was part of our daily rhythm.

For the first ten to twelve years of their lives, there was no TV and there were no films or electronic devices; their imaginations were fired by books. We spent a lot of time outdoors and did some quite old-fashioned activities such as kite flying, fishing, camping, archery, skateboarding, kite karting, kneeboarding, wakeboarding, water skiing, swimming and a host of adventurous confidence-building pursuits.

When they were growing up, the children were quite easygoing and happy to engage in water sports and fishing, the activities I loved. Our family almost always had a dog, which gave the children a great deal of fun and delight. Much comfort was felt and a tangible love revealed, in having such an affectionate pet; and inevitably of course, great sadness at their passing. Each child had their particular interests and William was always very musical. From an early age, he spent his free time writing poetry and music and playing instruments, performing his own songs featuring positive messages for young people. James was a Grade 8 violinist and Oliver was a Grade 6 violinist, both playing in the school orchestra. Natasha was popular and outgoing; a people person, with her life centring on supporting friends and helping those in need.

There is worldwide concern about the dangers of children becoming reliant on, and addicted to, social media and the internet. In addition,

I'm particularly concerned about the cognitive damage done by exposure to any frightening material too young in life before children are able to choose what is and is not appropriate. This can come from books, films, TV and the internet. If small children engage with something they don't understand and which alarms or scares them, the trauma of this can cause a blockage or decline in their natural cognitive abilities – in other words their vulnerable minds become too patterned with fear to be able to think clearly.

Even such popular childhood staples as Grimm's fairy tales can, in my opinion, have a negative developmental effect if children have access to them at too early an age. It really goes back to the age-old adage that before children are left to freely choose, they should have reached maturity, and before that stage, they need to be guided by knowledgeable parents and teachers. This is a problem in today's world, as the early foundations of inappropriate and 'child-unfriendly' information can take a lifetime to process and resolve, even requiring some form of mental health therapy in later life.

At one point, I wrote a blog about these misgivings and included some well-known children's books in my list of the sort of potentially frightening material that might be detrimental to children's healthy development if they were exposed to it at too young an age. Somehow, the press got hold of it, and to my surprise the piece was picked up and covered by newspapers in several countries around the world, causing some furore. Unfortunately, they either misread or misrepresented my statement, reporting sensationally that I was attacking children's literature – instead of recounting that I was only suggesting caution as to the age at which it is appropriate for children to have access to scary stories.

I received a large number of comments, some of which were in agreement with my views, but many of which were outraged by their misperception that I was negatively criticising popular childhood culture. It was mortifying that the prolonged fracas led to some unpleasant fallout and disturbance for my long-suffering family over the following year. I'm still in touch with some of the people who responded to my viewpoint, and they share my concern that exposure to terrifying or horrifying tales in any medium at too early an age, might indeed lead to problems in later life.

A headteacher working the long hours that it takes to run a school and train the staff, needs fun things to do, and my lifetime's passion for fishing was my main relaxation. Following on from my earlier carp fishing days, I continued to fly fish for trout and salmon, often with Barney Franklin, who later became Acorn headteacher. We went on fishing expeditions to lakes and rivers and then out to sea every summer, catching mackerel. We caught a lot of fish and those fishing trips were my Shangri-La.

I also spent many hours in my spare time hand building and restoring boats. Since 1980 I have bought and restored about twenty-five sports and sailing boats, and latterly I acquired super speedboats which the children all enjoyed and which helped them to become proficient at water sports. We shared these boats throughout the year with friends and Acorn students.

Since the 1970s archery has been another favourite leisure pursuit, and I've constructed many bows, even making and fletching my own arrows. At Kings Langley I produced some longbows, and it was an excellent fun activity for me to do with the children. I shot nationally at that time, with both recurve bows and longbows, and I eventually became a compound bow archer, doing quite well in competitions. I also brought my love of air rifle shooting to the Acorn students, and this was a sport everyone enjoyed, especially on our camps – where I have to admit that Sarah was often the best shot!

One evening on a winter camp, just for fun, I wanted to prove that archery was a better sport than air rifle shooting. So Barney and I organised an indoor archery and rifle range, and I set up and lit six candles at 20 metres. I shot at the candles one by one and snuffed each candle out with an arrow, shooting through each flame and never hitting a candle. I also split a page of The Times in half with an arrow, which the children then all wanted to do too. They discovered that these feats could only be accomplished with a bow and arrow, but not with an air rifle.

With long hours at school, bringing up my family, fishing, boat building and other pastimes, I enjoyed the adventure of my full life. It reminded me of how my father had lived – always doing interesting things and invariably having a project or three on the go. However, at the centre of all this activity, my attention was continually focusing on what the school's pupils needed most and what was best for my family.

Looking at what helps children to thrive, I think it is crucial that each child is truly seen, rather than being stuck behind a label, as I was at school when I was pigeonholed as 'another war child'. Consequently, my approach to schooling offers education on an individual basis, where children can be educated in a relaxed and stress-free non-competitive environment and be seen as the individuals they are throughout their entire education. To build this into the system, The Acorn School usually has only between ten and fifteen students in a class, enabling the teacher to give each child the individual attention they deserve.

Given my own painful experiences at school, I see kindness towards all students as an essential ingredient of school life, and Acorn has zero tolerance for any sort of unkind behaviour. As far as I'm aware there is no bullying at the school. Any unkindness or unacceptable behaviour is dealt with very quickly, and the school's performance in this area has earned considerable praise from parents and Ofsted. When new children enter Acorn for their trial period, they are each paired with an already-established older student who becomes their special buddy. The buddy acts like an interested and kind older sibling who can look out for the new arrival and help them with any concerns they may have about the school. This fosters a sense of worth and belonging in the new student, a sense of caring and responsibility in the older one, and a feeling of family throughout the school.

Having learnt from my unforgettable schoolboy encounters with chastisement, there is no formal punishment at The Acorn School and no detention. Discipline, derived from the word 'disciple', is achieved by example. I believe that by setting the right loving, caring and professional example, children can relax into learning with joy and complete engagement, all of which occurs naturally in our child-centred school.

I remember my father once standing outside my junior school, too nervous to enter due to his feelings of shame about his injured leg. That incident caused me considerable distress and stuck in my mind, so that when I later became a teacher, I wanted every parent to be welcomed and accepted into the schools where I taught. Hence, at Acorn, parents are encouraged to be involved and included in many activities such as school assemblies, school plays, choir and musical events, as well as community meetings for specific festivals eg Whitsun, Harvest, Martinmas, Advent and Christmas. Each week begins with a whole school assembly for all parents and children, bringing the Acorn community together on a weekly basis.

Another aspect of Acorn's community life that has been enriching for both the school and our family, is the twinning of The Acorn School with The Waldorf School in Überlingen, Germany. A visiting scheme ran for several years, under which a few upper school pupils from Germany would come over each year to study at Acorn for one to three terms. During their few months stay in the UK, the German teenagers lived with Sarah and me in our family home. We must have hosted about fifty German students in all, and this interchange was always beneficial for the school and the visitors.

Again arising from my own experiences at school, it is important to me that each student leaves the school feeling seen and acknowledged for who they are. When students graduate from Acorn, there is a special evening to honour each one and give them an encouraging send-off. It's a black tie, formal event for which everyone dresses up in their best, and to which all parents of the graduating students, and the staff and upper school students are invited. The parents prepare a magnificent feast which is served by students a class or two below those graduating. This is followed by some music performed by the students. Each graduate makes a short speech about their time at Acorn, usually including much humour and some emotion, and the headteacher responds to each one with appreciation for the particular qualities shown by the graduating student. It is a moving and affirming event that creates a positive finale to the students' time at Acorn and sends them on to their next venture with the knowledge that they are valued individuals with much to offer the world.

In 2001, ten years after the school was founded, and when our youngest, Oliver, entered Class 1 at Acorn, aged seven, Sarah expressed her wish to return to teaching and to work with me at the school. So when Oliver was in the Lower school, Sarah became a class teacher, continuing to excel in this role for the next twenty years. As we were both then working at Acorn, in 2003 we moved from Stroud to Nailsworth in order to be closer to school. And in 2008 we moved to our current home, an old farmhouse just outside Nailsworth and only a five minute drive from the school.

Thanks to the ingenuity and flexibility of the staff and parents, in the midst of the 2020-21 coronavirus COVID-19 pandemic, when much of our society went into some form of lockdown, our school remained open. We were able to continue with our education by temporarily extending the use of online facilities, ensuring that the children could receive their schooling without such serious worldwide situations impinging on their development.

To encourage students to enjoy this new form of learning during the pandemic lockdown, I started my online pre-main lesson period by playing folk songs on my guitar. This is how younger pupils have always learned to love what is coming in the upper school, when they go away on adventure camps, and the campfire is the centre of their social gatherings. They still ask for some of the great hits from the 1960s, particularly Leaving on a Jet Plane; and one of the school's favourite songs has been Another Man's Cause by The Levellers which is about the Falklands War.

Folk guitar has been an important and central part of Acorn's culture. I have taught guitar to a number of pupils at the school, and it has not been unusual for me to pick up my guitar during a lesson whilst my students are drawing or writing, and sing and play folk songs. Indeed, many times they have asked me, in their usual polite way,

'Graeme, if we are all working well, can you play and sing to us, please?'

As well as tutoring in music, the school prides itself on teaching a vast array or practical crafts, from general woodwork to toy making, carving, construction and many more complex activities such as coracle and canoe making. Children may learn how to make musical instruments eg a cello, a guitar, or something to enhance their enjoyment of a favourite pastime or as a gift for others. I feel it is important to recognise that talent comes in many guises, not just the academic. Finding the pleasure in developing new skills in diverse areas is one of the keys to uncovering hidden potential.


Team sports aren't offered at Acorn as there aren't sufficient facilities, and the competition involved doesn't suit the school's ethos. I don't consider the competitive pressure and resulting exclusion to be the most sensible way of educating children; though many children at the school do engage in team sports outside of school hours. I'm also aware of the dangers inherent in contact sports such as football, rugby and boxing, which can lead to some serious medical conditions later on. However, the school's physical education and outward-bound curriculum is second-to-none and has stood on its own as completely revolutionary.

For twenty-five years we have offered ski trips to Austria, which have proved popular with the senior students. These were suspended due to the coronavirus lockdown, but will resume as soon as possible. Sarah has come on some of these ski trips and been closely involved in organising and running a large number of outward bound trips and camps. During our times away she has often been the adult responsible for looking after the girls, while demonstrating her culinary skills in all sorts of challenging situations.

Swim School has been a feature of the school since the beginning. Following my competitive swimming days back in the army, I've taught swimming for over fifty years and in 2022 I still teach it, together with Sarah and Oliver. The after-school lessons at Acorn's Swim School are based on my own methodology which is not competitive. My aim is for the children to enjoy being in the water and to be safe, without always needing to compete.

As the school grew, I introduced water skiing, knee-boarding and wakeboarding, along with the sports boats, sailing boats and Canadian canoes that we took on our trips. Every year, for as long as I was able, I took the upper school students on a tour to Italy and France in connection with the history of art. These trips were iconic and I have many fond memories of the students' faces as they stood before some of the world's greatest works of art. I'm opposed to the critical assessment of children's art, preferring their artworks to be seen in their pure breathtaking reality, so that students can form their own impressions rather than being presented with any adult's intellectual view. Those who have gone on to study the history of art at university have had plenty of opportunity to receive critical appraisal!

Our own children engaged at some stage with all of these activities. When they were younger, it was a case of them watching their father take off, either at home or abroad, with other people's children. This prepared the ground for when they got older and were able to fully take part and have fun on the trips.

I asked Barney, my former student and later Acorn headteacher, to give his own account of some of the school's outdoor activities and trips:

### Summer Camps

*My first experiences of Acorn outdoor trips were the summer camps that Graeme used to run down in South Devon. I was a young teenage boy with a thirst for adventure, and these camps certainly gave me that. By the age of 15, Graeme had already put me in charge of one of the boats we would take out to sea from Salcombe harbour with the many students that joined the camps from a number of Steiner schools around the country. Graeme would introduce the children to a wide range of exciting activities that they lapped up with great enthusiasm.*

*Rock jumping was extremely popular with jumps being attempted way above 20 feet. This activity is now called 'coasteering' in outdoor pursuits centres, but Graeme was doing it 30 years before it became recognised. We would motor around the coast looking for likely spots, and then if one was found, swim in and check the depth. If it seemed suitable then one of us would scramble up the cliff to a selected ledge and take a leap of faith. If all went well then the jump was named, and the students could start jumping. I remember two jumps in particular: The Big Beast and Heaven!*

*Another activity was anchor jumping. The idea was simple. You took a boat out into about 20 feet of water and then jumped off it wearing a mask and holding an anchor. It's amazing how fast you go to the bottom. Once down there you have a short while to observe any marine life that might be lurking in the depths before you run out of air and head to the surface.*

*Boat jumping was another fun activity. Graeme would drive the boat a good way offshore and then have the students stand on the side of the boat while it was still moving at a moderate speed. The command was then given to jump. This in itself was exhilarating, but the activity became more exciting still when the boat disappeared over the waves, and you were left with your friends in the wide expanse of ocean. Hands were held and a circle formed, and together you conquered your fears.*

*Wave jumping was also great fun. This involved bouncing in a high-powered speed boat over the large mountains of water that surge into Salcombe harbour. It's quite a feeling to know that the boat is completely out of the water apart from the propeller.*

*The days were also filled with snorkelling, canoeing, surfing, knee boarding and power boarding – a great invention of Graeme's. He took a 12 foot windsurfer and drilled a hole in the front. A ski rope was attached to it and the other end tied to the speed boat. A number of students would clamber on the board and hang on for dear life as Graeme drove off at speed, trying to make them fall off. It was immense fun and the main reason people fell off was because they were laughing so much. I remember one time towing Graeme and another student, and whilst travelling at 20 mph Graeme got the student to stand on his shoulders!*

### Canoeing

*Canoeing trips have always been a big part of the Acorn outdoor experiences. Part of the magic of the early ones was that the students had actually made the canoes themselves in school. I remember the first trip I went on with the school was when I was back on Christmas leave from the army, and Graeme convinced me it was a good idea to take a group of students on a two-night expedition down the River Wye. We set off on New Year's Day with frost coating the banks and mist hanging over the freezing water. This trip was done with basic equipment, with students cooking on simple Trangia cookers and sleeping in survival bags. There was no plan in place, we just paddled till dusk and then began to look for likely wild places on the bank where we could tuck ourselves away for the night. A fire would always be lit and stories would be told, with song suggestions flowing late into the night. Night games were always played too. Escape and evasion, storm the fort and torch tag to name a few. After a few days on the river, a suitable exit point would be chosen, and then someone would head off to find a telephone box to tell a willing parent where we had got to, so they could come and pick us up.*

*Over the many years we began to know the river really well and even started to name the places where we stayed. There was Fir Tree Camp, Castle Camp, Badger Camp, Capsize Camp and Red Cliff Camp to name a few. Landowners didn't always appreciate our covert visits, but Graeme invariably had a story up his sleeve that would usually manage to appeal to their better nature.*

## Mountain Expeditions

*My first mountain expedition with Graeme was in 1996 when we took the older Acorn students on a 12-day trip to the Isle of Skye. We loaded everyone into two minibuses and headed north. We knew what island we were heading to but that was all. The trip was all about spontaneity. We explored the island and wild camped by rivers and lakes, often high in the mountains. We caught fish and ate them, and Graeme had also brought along a few air rifles, so we shot some rabbits and taught the students how to skin and cook them. It rained for most of the trip and we were plagued with midges. But even though the trip was tough, the students rose to it and learned a great deal about improvising, adapting and overcoming adversity.*

*On another trip, we were taking a group walking in the Lake District, and we'd got halfway up there when Graeme heard on the radio that the weather was pretty rough. So he turned left at the next junction and headed for north Wales with the plan of searching out a spot he remembered from his days on an army training exercise.*

*We arrived at the base of a mountain called Cader Idris and were soon heading up its steep slopes. Evening was falling fast, and we spotted a dense conifer forest up ahead. We fought our way into the centre of it and found a wonderful spot to rough camp. Soon, a fire was lit and food was cooked. I remember the following morning, climbing up to a freezing cold mountain lake and all of the students leaping in for a swim before we headed for the summit.*

*Singing around the campfire in the evenings was a huge part of these trips. It was something the students loved; and the fact that we might be halfway up a mountain or paddling down a fast-flowing river swollen with winter floodwater never stopped Graeme from bringing along his trusty guitar.*

*Over many years, Graeme led mountain expeditions all around the UK and Ireland. All of these trips gave the students a real sense of adventure and excitement. They learnt how to be responsible for their kit and themselves; how to be respectful to nature and experience the seriousness of bad weather. Graeme believed very strongly that through these unique experiences, exceptional groups could be formed and important life lessons taught that couldn't possibly be accomplished in the classroom.*

*These trips were never micromanaged, and although safety was paramount, students were never wrapped in cotton wool. Instilling in the students some fundamental practical life skills and giving them numerous opportunities to problem solve and use their common sense really allowed them to experience the outdoor world in a real way rather than as the no-risk sanitised versions that are often expected to inspire young people today.*

## *The Italy Trip*

*Nothing has shown better than the Acorn History of Art Trip that for education to really be meaningful for young people, they must not only learn in the classroom but also experience what they have learnt out in the real world. Graeme has run around 15 of these and they involve the students heading off on a 3,500-mile journey across France, through the Alps and around Italy, taking in Venice, Assisi, Rome, Naples, Siena, Florence and Pisa. The final part of the trip involves a drive along the French Riviera and then back up through central France, stopping in Paris on the way. Finally, there is a visit to the WW1 war graves before heading for home.*

*All this is undertaken in the school minibus with students sleeping in tents and doing their own cooking over camping stoves. The route is flexible and can change from year to year. If a nice-looking Italian town is spotted high up in the hills then it's added to the itinerary and the students all keep an eye out of the window for camping signs. I remember once when no campsite was found, Graeme bivvied the students up in a nearby forest for the night and we rough camped.*

*The trips have always been full of adventure and there have been many times when things didn't go to plan. A number of trips have had to deal with mechanical issues in the minibus. One of the most notable involved the minibus breaking down halfway up Mt Vesuvius. Graeme stayed with the students in the lay-by we had pulled into, which was by an abandoned house riddled with bullet holes. I hitched down to the local village, clutching an Italian phrasebook. A mechanic was found, and our minibus was rolled down the hill into his driveway. That night we all slept in his garage whilst he worked through the night. By the morning he told us it was all fixed, and we handed him a large sum of money and loaded the students back on board. A nightmare at the time, but looking back on it, a wonderful opportunity for the students to experience life when things are not always going perfectly.*

*The Italy trip is between 2 and 3 weeks long and is the one trip that students always look back on not only as superb fun but also as something that really helped them in later life with regards to the skills they learned. I believe that the Italy trip that Graeme created is one of a kind and really pushes the boundaries of what is possible in education. Trips such as this have become more and more rare in the modern world; a shame as they are so beneficial to young people.*

This is a time when government propriety has curtailed many of the adventurous activities the children have undertaken in the past, and the Health and Safety Executive has certainly contributed to a general lack of fitness in children. In many respects it has pushed young people towards seeking adventures on screens in their bedrooms; a propensity from which I'm pleased to exempt the children in my school, at least to some degree.

It's important to make clear that all of our water sports, outdoor pursuits and other physical activities have only been possible at Acorn because of the highly trained and disciplined nature of the staff. Safety is paramount. My many years as an instructor in the army gave me the high level training and experience to be able to safely initiate and supervise a whole range of physical activities. It would be dangerous and indefensible for anyone with insufficient training and experience to attempt to organise any exercises that involve risk. At Acorn I have been ably assisted by Barney and my sons, James and Oliver – all suitably trained in the fields of physical education or outward bound.

Sarah has always been beside me, co-creating Acorn, and whatever has been achieved, we've achieved together. Sarah's early experiences, firstly in prep school and then in a Steiner school, have interwoven with my own and formed our joint approach to education. From September 2022 she will be co-headteacher of Acorn, sharing the headship with another member of staff, while Barney resumes teaching gym. Sarah also plays a core role in Acorn's life as the unofficial mother of the school – she embraces and nurtures the whole community, respected by the parent group and loved by the children, past and present.

Our son, James, made a six-year commitment to the school and became headteacher for three of them. Working very hard for all those years, James brought Acorn through a foggy mist to make it ready for essential new growth, befitting the modern world. He has steered the school through the haze of new educational requirements, the world of tick boxes, and has been a superb and highly respected natural leader.

The school has passed its thirtieth year and we have much to celebrate. I am aware that the Acorn I founded, although still functional and a great school, has had its free educational philosophy curbed, particularly in respect of the school's physical education and outdoor activities. It is a real fight to maintain pure education in the face of state controls and requirements. Nonetheless, Acorn is a cutting-edge place to be educated and we rely on the support and commitment of our magnificent parent body to continue to demonstrate that some alternatives to state-provided education are thriving.

In my twenty-seven years creating and running the school, I went through a great struggle, but I was able to generate my golden chalice. It has subsequently been necessary for me to take a step back from my original school plan, to allow Acorn to evolve with the times and move forward with new teachers. I've found this quite difficult, but I do my best not to constrain the school from finding new directions. I still teach some of the main lessons which are such a key feature of the school, and Sarah's new role as co-headteacher puts her at the centre of Acorn's pastoral care. Sarah and I also have a presence in the school as its owners, and we are focused on keeping the heart and spirit of Acorn alive and burning bright.

The Acorn School is successfully challenging the status quo, and over the last thirty years, every Acorn student who has chosen to further their studies at university has secured a place without taking any exams. Following the adoption of teacher assessment instead of exams during the 2021 coronavirus pandemic, it would be rewarding to see the government finally show some sense regarding the ability of teachers to be trusted as the professionals who should assess which children can enter higher education or other pathways. But the state exam system returned in 2022, and perhaps it will take decades for such crass and unimaginative exams as GCSEs and A-levels to be scrapped in favour of a continuous assessment system akin to the internationally accepted New Zealand Certificate of Steiner Education now used at Acorn.

I don't assess my vision by the number of university places achieved, or the levels of degrees attained from taking the Acorn path but by the quality of the human beings who enter the adult world. I'm so pleased that we have a school where moral values, the pursuit of knowledge and upholding one's right to become a freethinking adult is our educational vision and the target of all the students.

Acorn graduates have been taught to recognise their capabilities and to be ready to walk the road less travelled, to challenge the road often travelled, to embrace society, and to follow their heart and realise their potential. The Acorn School is now confidently moving forward into the next decade, continuing to ensure that its young people receive an education which treats them all as distinctively individual children, enabling them to then find their place in society as unique adults.

# CHAPTER 14

# REFLECTIONS

Looking back and considering all the hardships I suffered and the struggles I underwent, I feel that I have managed to accomplish my dreams and realise my potential – the potential that only one teacher saw many years ago as he cast his eye over the waif-like war child standing in front of him. But at the age of seventy-eight, I still have a lot to do in order to continue to develop my vision of education. I want to continue to challenge the modern world's mentality which seeks to transform human beings, especially children, into something other than what I feel is appropriate.

Does this new digital world aim to turn children into automatons by the time they become young adults? Ironically, this fast-moving world has recently been stricken by an ever-mutating coronavirus, at times being brought to a virtual standstill whilst we struggle to find a way past the invisible assailant. It's extraordinary that the world can change so much through the power of something we can't see, but which can be replicated thousands of times in a single cell. Other powers that can't be seen and which have infected humanity, are the internet and smartphones, which people have been subliminally encouraged to think they need as though they were as essential as food. But are they?

Despite the virus, I can see a different world, a world of beautiful countryside, ecstatic skyscapes, awesome and bountiful night skies, staggering mountain ranges, and a world rich with individually unique and wonderful people. Human beings should not look into the darkness without seeing light and should not look into the light without seeing darkness. I have learned to love and respect our exquisite world in all of its facets.

Some time ago, on a spring walk through fields of rippling, green grass, down tiny, twisting shady lanes with a morning breeze and the birds abounding with an unusual busyness, I was overtaken by some fast-pedalling young lads on their bikes. I saw them turn into a gateway and heard their shouts of joy when they saw the magnificence of the lake in the early spring morning. When I arrived at the gate, I watched them stealthily make their way along a narrow path by the water, prodding here and there as they investigated everything that looked interesting. I was pleased to see these youngsters savouring the delights of nature as I'd done all those years ago when I was a boy.

They clearly thought they knew a bit about the inhabitants of the lake as I heard them mention pike and tench and bream. Stopping at a patch of lilies, they carefully positioned their landing net underneath a dark shape they'd spotted among the lily pads, and after a few seconds they landed a big fish on the bank. They were excitedly jumping about and marvelling at the floundering creature when I appeared on the scene. I saw the beautiful fish lying helplessly on the ground, gasping for air, so I picked it up and returned it to the water as the boys looked on in awe. I told them it was a common carp of about 8 lbs and explained that it was wrong to heave it out of the water in the way that they had. They looked down and seemed upset as I told them that they should have been content to watch it from the bank.

From the expressions on their faces, it was obvious they were full of remorse, and I understood their actions and knew they'd never seen anything like that carp before; they couldn't resist the chance to look at it more closely and had done what any young lads would do in the circumstances. I could see they had a love of nature and the countryside. We talked about carp for a while, and they were interested to know more, claiming that it was now their intention to catch fish with the proper gear, and they would meet me there again when they'd got their new kit. I heard that they'd previously met a couple of regular carp anglers at the lake, who had no interest in helping these young boys to appreciate the art of fishing and had even been openly hostile to their presence there.

My next visit to the lake coincided with the lads' first trip with their new equipment, which was excellent and would allow them a reasonable chance of catching carp. To their delight, I showed them my buzzer and some other modern-day gimmicks for the dedicated carp angler, and I knew they'd never forget this introduction to the intricacies and wonders of serious carp fishing.

Fast forward to recently, and on my last visit to the lake I was pleased to walk around to where I recognised two very ardent and now grown-up carp anglers. They had all the best gear; we talked of recent experiences and they even gave me some advice! I know that similar meetings take place all over the country each summer, and as a result boys become men and men become responsible and caring anglers. Prudent advice and giving the right messages about fishing etiquette to young budding anglers is vital for the future of the sport. I was pleased that I had been able to help these young lads grow up to fully enjoy the pleasures of fishing in the finest way.


You know the story about the man who found happiness in everything, every day of his life, the man who woke up every morning seeking the thrill that the day would offer him? Well, I am that man, and every day I feel that my life is fulfilled. The pathway of everyone's life is an individual secret that will have a different meaning for each person. The pinnacle of the human task is to reach that secret to happiness in each child. My secret is 'taking the road less travelled' and following one's heart.

Taking the road less travelled includes a way of facing difficulties and feeling at one with oneself. It is a childhood path that I want to teach, to help children see the beautiful world as I see it. In knowing our world, in seeing what it has become and imagining what it could become again, I perceive that the key to the future of mankind lies in the adoption of humane values, in creating a strong and loving family and a world where children are encouraged to explore and take risks to enable their individuality to flourish. And above all, an education that meets the needs and honours the potential of every individual child, instead of a system where children are encouraged to compete against each other.

I remember much, if not the majority, of what I was taught at school, and I have often looked back and used that knowledge as I taught a myriad of subjects. Life is often about what we learned in earlier years and although many hurtful things happened to me during my years at school – bullying, criticism, teasing and corporal punishment – I have worked hard to overcome those things.

Such times taught me many lessons, and the principal one is that what takes place in one's life helps one to know who one is. At the times of un-kindness, I was upset and cried a lot, but on reflection, when I look around today, I see a world that is a lot worse in many ways for children growing up now than it was when I was a child. The current 'unsocial' media have had some sad effects on today's young people, and I am so pleased that I climbed trees, scrumped apples from the parson's garden, played around and spent time outdoors with my friends, instead of being encapsulated in a bedroom full of junk and the electronic must-haves that now litter the bedrooms of many children. I am happy that I had the opportunity to teach my children as I saw fit, ensuring that they have a host of interesting and exciting stories to remember from their schooldays.

Another thing I've learned is that we don't get asked many questions by our children when they are young, no matter how keen we are to tell them. They know us better than anyone else, and I guess it is the same in all families. It is not until later that they ask and are ready to hear about their parents' life, and one must never push it upon them. There is always time, and as our children are a reflection of their upbringing and our parenting, we may be hopeful that one day they will be ready to listen and ask questions.

Yesterday, I called my oldest sister, Joan, for the umpteenth time to speak about the past, our mum and dad, grandad and grandma, to ensure that I can pass down their stories before it is too late. Luckily, there have been no family rifts and we've all been able to respect that we are very different and sometimes strongly opinionated people. I have now lost my parents, four of my brothers, Bill, John, Reg and Mick and one of my sisters, Kim, but I often still reflect on the rich and accomplished lives of my siblings. Although my wider family were distant, my relationships with my eight brothers and sisters have always been important to me.

Bill, the oldest and my childhood hero, spent his life committed to carp angling and was an excellent pianist with a love of classical music. He wrote poetry and published three books under the name of William Wynn Whiting. With our shared interests in fishing, motorbikes, literature and music, we stayed close as adults. When he was later struggling with an illness almost certainly brought on by his lifelong smoking, I fulfilled one of his ambitions to stand in Rydal Mount and read 'Daffodils' by William Wordsworth; I read the poem to him on my mobile phone as he listened at home in tears. When he was near the end and in hospital, I sent him a letter containing these words: 'Look behind you my big bro. There, by the curtains you will see me standing looking over you. Never, ever think I am not there, bro. I will watch you as you lift this dark curtain and look back on the richness of your life.' My last words to him were about fishing, and indeed, in a loving gesture, his friends arranged for a massive carp to be swimming in the pond outside the crematorium. After his death in 2006, we discovered that Bill had led a secret double life, having had a relationship outside his marriage for many years. The revelation didn't detract from my love and respect for him, and his death was a heavy blow to me.

Joan, my oldest sister, is ninety-one years old as I write and a wise, caring woman with a strong Christian ethos who raised a family of three together with her dear husband. They had an exciting life, living in North Africa and Germany where they moved due to her husband's work for The Meteorological Office. He died in 1982, so she has been on her own for forty years, during which time we've remained close. She is a kind and thoughtful older sister and we still speak every few days. Joan is now the head of the family and often reminds me of the time when I was on reins in Norfolk and she had to change my nappy!

John was a superb teacher and an exceptional canoeist and swimmer, often away on trips with his students. We were both physical educationists and teachers and I looked up to him, but we weren't close; though I did illustrate one of his books, and while I was in the army I was a guinea pig in some physical training experiments for his PhD. In the early 1970s he encouraged me to try for a scholarship to Oxford, while he and his wife offered to look after Maxine until I'd completed my degree; an incredibly kind offer that I sadly wasn't able to take up. John was the founder of Human Movement Science, a fellow of the British Psychological Society and founder of The British Society of Sport Psychology, with numerous other qualifications including being an honorary Colonel in the Canadian Air Force and an honorary Sheriff of Dallas County! His sudden death in 2001 was a shock to the whole family.

After being distant during my childhood, Reg and I found one another after my army service, and that relationship thrived until he died in 2016. He was a devoted family man and worked in a law practice until his retirement. He spent his spare time caring for those less fortunate than him, making a commitment to helping disabled people and walking the wounded and the infirm in their wheelchairs along the seaside promenade at Gorleston-on-Sea. I was proud of him, and we were close for the last ten years of his life; when he was in hospital I sent him the same message I had sent to Bill.

Kim, my second oldest sister, committed her life to education, owning a Montessori School in London and being crowned 'Montessorian of the Year' in 2006. She also practised as a professional counsellor for many years. Kim was a highly intelligent and knowledgeable woman with an interest in alternative approaches to the world. She overcame cancer twice, but finally succumbed to the disease and died in 2021. As mentioned, she was key in my having turned to the Steiner system of education, and for the last ten years of her life we had a particularly strong connection. For a while until shortly before her death, I spoke to Kim every day, and we frequently debated education and politics, sometimes in agreement though often not. Our conversations were forthright and intellectually challenging, and her passion and sharpness of mind were an inspiration. I miss her terribly.

When I was in the army, I finally gained approval from Mick, the wayward older brother who had teased me so mercilessly as a teenager. One day he was beaten up by a rival gang member, and as he picked himself up, Mick threatened that when his big, strong brother came home on army leave he would sort this rival out. I returned and did the deed, and Mick and I became friends, staying in touch until his death. In contrast to his early headstrong years, I found him to be an intelligent and caring man; and he actually wrote me a letter asking if I could forgive him for tormenting me when we were children, which of course I did. He had his own printing business and lived for most of his adult life with his wife and three children in New Zealand where he discovered an affinity with the Maoris. Always a great dancer, Mick had a passion for Elvis Presley, and when I visited him shortly before he died, I saw that the walls of his house were covered with Elvis pictures. A sensitive and much-valued brother, he was a central figure in the family. Mick died from cancer in 2017.

David, the brother above me by three years, is another intelligent and successful family man. When the 'open door' policy adopted by the government encouraged so many to leave the UK, David travelled to

New Zealand where he settled for many decades near Mick. Continuing his love of cranes, he started his own crane business which did very well, and he later moved to Perth in Western Australia, where he managed a large crane company. David recently retired, after which he has become a cruise enthusiast, travelling around the world with his wife, who happened to be in my age group at school. A newfound relationship has brought us very close in our seventies; we talk every few days, and as the only two boys left, I feel we are somewhat joined at the hip!

My younger sister and childhood best friend, Dawn, married early and left the UK for a new life in Canada over fifty years ago. We drifted apart for a while after she emigrated, partly because her husband was not what he seemed to be when she first knew him, and the marriage soon ended. She stayed in British Columbia with her three children, and she is a dedicated mother with a firm Christian faith; but her life has not been easy. I remember how she stood by my side through times of great hardship, and she remains a loving sibling. We are as close now as when we were children, and I speak to Dawn every day or two.


After struggling for so much of my life, I feel blessed to have a loving wife, five children and now our two grandchildren, all living within easy reach. Our current dog is a Schnauzer called Freida, an adored member of the family. We saved her from a breeder who didn't want her because her underbite meant she couldn't compete in dog shows, and she has proved to be a treasure.

For some years Maxine continued to live in Bristol and then moved to Devon where her daughter, Talia, was born in 2003. They later moved back to Bristol and have stayed in close contact with the rest of the family. William, Natasha, James and Oliver all completed their schooling at Acorn. William then went to Stroud College in 2001, studying a course in Fine Art, and instead of taking up his university place, he chose to become a youth worker while continuing with his music. On leaving

Acorn, Natasha went straight to Thailand as a volunteer and set up a charity to support her work. James left school in 2011 to study Sports and Exercise Science at Loughborough University, following in my brother John's footsteps. And after Acorn Oliver went to the University of West of England at Hartpury to study sports coaching and for a while played semi-professional rugby for Cinderford.

As well as managing to create a successful school from my educational vision, I'm fortunate to have led an active and innovative life, including running several businesses and inventing useful devices; although mostly without the necessary funds to patent or bring them to production. Our finances were limited for so long, but when Sarah's father died, he left her some money and a house, which we used to bail out and support the school and which also gave us the opportunity to travel – a treat after years of just scraping by.

In 2000 Sarah and I and our four youngest children visited my brothers in New Zealand, while Maxine and her daughter went over in 2008. We were able to visit Natasha in Thailand, and over recent years I have enjoyed some overseas skiing and fishing trips, many of them with my close friend, Terry Oldfield. He is not only an outstanding musician and renowned composer, but also a first-class salmon fly fisherman who has taught me a great deal. When the school began to grow, and I was at last able to afford such luxuries, we used to ski together every year on a glacier in Austria and have fished in endless lakes and rivers. In August 2022 we enjoyed our latest salmon fly fishing trip to Scotland, after the previous year's overseas trip was cancelled due to the coronavirus pandemic.

I am also privileged to be good friends with Jeremy Wade, one of the world's leading anglers and one of the nicest people I've ever met. As a former student of mine, he is one of the ex-pupils who have kindly allowed me to include their testimonials at the end of this book. Although there is only a twelve year age difference between us, I have a somewhat fatherly feeling towards him and look forward to future fishing trips and swapping angling stories. I've heard Jeremy say that he can't imagine my ever fully retiring – I can see his point!

In 2008, Sarah suggested I take Oliver to Madeira, an island in the Atlantic off West Africa, to fulfil one of my childhood dreams and see if we could catch a giant blue marlin. It was exhilarating to be out on a boat and watch the dolphins jumping, the whales breaching, and the sea alive with all kinds of fish and many giant turtles. Oliver was mesmerised by the breathtaking array of deep sea mysteries. For four days we scanned the water for baitfish and trawled on the stunning blue water, our short carbon fibre marlin rods ready in the stern.

Suddenly I saw a black fin standing proud on a dark blue shiny back about 40 metres behind the boat and travelling at the same speed. I shouted to the two men who were hiring out the boat, but they carried on drinking their beer and showed no interest as they clearly didn't believe their customer had seen something that they, the experts, had missed. Within a few minutes, I saw a huge marlin with wide open mouth strike at the squid we were trailing as bait. I grabbed the rod, and an extraordinary fight began. I was strapped into the fighting chair, but the bolts holding it down started to loosen, so one of the men held onto the chair as the giant fish continually dived and breached in its attempt to break free.

Oliver was filming and cheering me on while I was doing my best to ensure that I could make the catch and remove the hook so the marlin could live. An American boat was nearby and started to radio our crew, but I was keen to keep them away from us so they couldn't claim my prize. About thirty minutes into the fight, I felt one and then the second shoulder dislocate – I was fighting one of the giants of the sea with serious, incapacitating injuries. I increased the pressure on the fish, and fortunately for me, this move miraculously clicked each shoulder back into place. We fought on and on for what seemed like hours.

The marlin was so strong it was pulling the boat backwards and we were filling with water. I shouted to the crew to turn the steering wheel to the left, and suddenly the line went slack and the water drained out of the back of the boat. I could now see the magnificent head of the marlin with its sad eye and its fin flapping gently like a black sail. I felt a surge of guilt and an urge to turn the clock back a couple of hours; it would be my fault if it died. I wondered how I would feel if, like it, I was tricked and hauled along by a rope against my will. I promised never to stir such an incredible creature from its watery home again; this would be my only marlin.

The marlin was now wallowing alongside the boat, and one of the crew was able to slip a rope noose over its bill so it could be unhooked. They tagged the dorsal fin and measured its length which was roughly 4 metres. The scale they used made its weight about 450 kgs. I watched as it seemed to look directly at me, shake its head and then slowly dive back into the deep. Oliver and I were enthralled by the whole experience; and I vowed never to catch such a creature again. I was glad to hear that the marlin lived and was caught again five years later off Brazil, at an even greater weight.

In 2018, following years of intense activity, I decided it was time to have a break from full-time teaching and focus on various projects, including a collection of short stories and writing about parenting in the digital age, based on the model of parenting that Sarah and I created for our own children. During that two year rest from teaching full-time, I had the opportunity to do many things for myself, as well as to continue to uphold the school's principles and guide its direction as its owner, keeping it on track so that the original vision could be maintained.

As part of extending the reach of the Acorn ethos, I have from time to time acted as an unpaid education consultant to the founders of some other educational initiatives: The Aquila Upper School at The Ringwood Steiner School, The London Acorn School, and The Moray Acorn School (now Drumduan School). I am currently assisting the possible restarting of two schools that were closed by Ofsted, though these are both still at a confidential stage. I am mostly called in to assist by teachers from the other schools who know me and have seen online the results of Acorn's success. My role is to guide and advise, but not to take over or take on another school, as my prime commitments are to my family and to Acorn. I'm clear about my own educational ideals and principles so I don't interfere with any ethos with which I don't agree. I'm glad to have made my contribution to the schools I've mentioned and also to several training courses for would-be teachers.

In 2022 I'm again only teaching part-time at the school and am working a lot more in home education. I provide tutoring to individual Acorn pupils who would like some extra tuition in various subjects. These one-to-one teaching sessions are proving popular and productive and allow me to continue working in Acorn education in a more flexible way.

As I finish writing my story, I look back at so many events that shaped who I am. My family, my education, my army service, my more than fifty-six years as a teacher. The unstinting will to create my own school, founded on many experiences in my life, has been nourished and sustained by my children, all of whom I taught, with the youngest four educated at Acorn. If I look for something that explains how I found this strength as a very ordinary man, I think it is because I have had to face the many challenges mentioned in this book. None of the difficulties and setbacks I met were a waste of time; they all truly helped me and made me the person I am today. And since I was a young boy, listening to my father all those years ago, I've had the principle of kindness and the thread of the golden chalice running through my life. Its luminous image has lit me up from inside and kept me going through all the desperate straits and hard times.

In 1964, when I was nineteen, I spent two days in Rome after my time on active service in Cyprus.

I sat by the Pieta, running my fingers down the silky sheen of carved marble and feeling every beautifully carved curve that is Michelangelo's great masterpiece which stands in St. Peter's Church in Rome. I was reading a handout and when I finished, I gazed into the face of Mary and could feel her pain. The Pieta was carved by Michelangelo when he was a youth, and shows her son, Jesus, held lovingly in her arms after being taken down from the cross. This is what I read:

One day in Florence, 500 years ago, a huge piece of marble, which had been quarried in Carrara, was being towed through the streets of Florence to be taken to a great sculptor's studio in order to be carved.

Michelangelo, then a young artist, followed the cart and asked the owner if the marble was for sale. This huge piece of marble had taken three weeks to be cut out of the marble mountain. It was then dragged down the mountain by oxen and strong men to the port of Carrara, then hauled onto a ship which sailed south to the river Arno and finally unloaded at the end of its journey, near the Ponte Vecchio in Florence.

The struggle and injuries sustained during the quarrying and journey impressed the young Michelangelo, and he could see beyond the rough exterior of the block.

The owner of the marble was somewhat dissatisfied with its quality and offered it to Michelangelo, knowing that he was being paid by Pope Julius II to sculpt forty free-standing statues for his tomb. The block was sold to the young Michelangelo for a fair price that was agreed by the pope.

Michelangelo steered the cart towards his outside studio, and people gazed on this piece of marble in wonder. There was much talk as to why he had bought such an unattractive piece of marble, some asking Michelangelo the obvious question:

'Buonarroti, why did you want to buy such a rough piece of marble?'

'Ah. Can't you see what is inside this beautiful block? Moses is trapped in there; I will release him.'

The Moses statue stands in the Church of San Pietro in Vincoli, just above the Colosseum, as a symbol, the only sculpture to be finished for the tomb of Julius II.

I walked to the church and stood in front of the statue. Since that day, over fifty-five years ago, I have taken many hundreds of students to stand and look upon this great work of art, as I have done more than thirty times.

That block of marble gave me the idea to one day carve a school and release the potential of all the children who attend. I pay tribute to the people who dragged the cart, the parents of the school who never thought twice before taking the road less travelled.

If I have enabled young children to sit behind a desk, run around in the wild, light a fire and cook in nature, gaze on the wondrous world that is theirs to be cherished and protected, paddle a canoe down a stunning silver shimmering river in which salmon leap for joy, climb mountains, play in the snow, travel to see many of the wonders of the world, love and nurture those less fortunate than the children whose parents can pay high private school fees, and make a commitment to children who have relatively nothing – then I am content.


The most important thing in my life is to be a good husband and father, a good teacher and to set examples for my children, freeing them from feelings of despair with the modern and fast-changing world, so that they become greater than me. And they all are! I admire my children, and my greatest pride is that they are all kind people who have helped those less fortunate than themselves.

I taught Maxine at Kings Langley from 1974 to 1984, and she left school at eighteen. She was a popular classmate and did extremely well to suffer ten years of being taught physical education by her father; but I was privileged, she was a superb student and one of my best gymnasts.

Maxine travelled extensively in her twenties and spent five years living in Australia. She worked in publishing for several years, and alongside, became a health practitioner and healer. In 2021, at the age of fifty-five, she started a Journalism and Publishing degree which she is due to finish in two years. She is a strong and courageous woman, and I am proud of the way she has single-handedly brought up her lovely daughter Talia, my granddaughter, who has grown into a wonderful young woman.

William has a golden heart and has often walked the streets of London helping homeless people in the depths of winter. He is an excellent individualistic artist and could easily have taken up a career in art, perhaps achieving as much as his maternal grandfather who was a celebrated film production designer. However, William has chosen to focus on developing his song-writing and music production talents. He and his partner live next door to us on the same property, so we're blessed to see them daily.

Natasha left school in 2004 at just eighteen and went to Thailand to do voluntary work with the street children in Bangkok. After the devastating December 2004 tsunami she travelled south to assist those affected by the destruction, helping them to rebuild and re-home. Sarah, I and our three boys visited there in 2005 and attended a moving candlelit ceremony to celebrate the lives of those who had died in the tsunami. Following a trip home later that year Natasha returned to Thailand after a few months, having developed a love of the Thai language and culture. Alongside a friend, Natasha then took on a children's home, growing it from seven to forty-seven children. She devoted her young life to giving these destitute children a life worth living and worked hard to raise money, funding the project until 2018 with the financial support of The Acorn School and the charity she set up, Acorn Overseas. The orphanage in Mae Sot became Natasha's golden chalice – a truly remarkable feat for one so young. For this achievement, she was named 2005 Young Person of The Year by Stroud District Council. Natasha has returned to the UK and is now living in London and working as founder and CEO of a premier health supplement company.

James is currently studying medicine as his second degree, after his six years of teaching at the school, with three of them as headteacher. He has truly earned this step after sacrificing his valuable time to get the school back on track after a slight dip in 2016. I owe James so much for what he has given to the school and to the many children he has guided into their adult life. Despite his incredibly busy schedule as a trainee doctor, he still plays a vital role at Acorn as the guardian of the school and Chairman of The Board.

In March 2020 James and his wife gave Sarah and me our second grandchild – a sweet boy called Leo, who we have the pleasure of seeing regularly as they live not far from us. Spending time with Leo reminds me how important it is to let young children explore activities and their surroundings in their own way and at their own pace, with the adult just providing materials and a loving space in which the child knows it's safe.

We're looking forward to extending our grandparenting as two more grandchildren are due to arrive in the autumn of 2022. William and his partner, Karolina, are expecting a girl in November, and James and his wife, Emily, are expecting a second boy in December. As Sarah and I will both be working part-time at the school, we're delighted to be able to spend time with these welcome additions to the family.

Oliver is uniquely talented and proficient in many sports and he has given his all to Acorn, both as pupil and teacher. Following his degree and a period playing semi-professional rugby, he returned to Acorn to take on the job of physical education teacher, specialising in outward bound, mountain leadership and climbing. In February 2022, after five years as an outstanding teacher and role model at the school, he began studying paramedic science at The University of the West of England as his second degree.

There is so much I could write about my children, but perhaps it is enough to say that I can sit back and enjoy the rest of my life in the knowledge that each one of them has found their own golden chalice within themselves. And I know that I am beholden to all five children for my own golden chalice, The Acorn School.

What we do in our lives as we grow towards adulthood, the many adventures in which we are involved, the challenges we face, the ups and downs we go through, the myriad of imagined experiences and the opportunities we're given to help those less fortunate than ourselves, all contribute to the path we take and our understanding of how privileged we are.

Each human being has a golden chalice within, but some have not yet realised it and some may still need to find it. My educational vision is that every child has potential, is an individual, and has the seeds within them to achieve whatever they wish. The challenge of education is to lift that potential towards reality. And the ability to help others and to see each human being as a unique individual is a reflection of our whole upbringing – including our education.

Every child has the right to receive an education that honours their potential. I can sum up my approach to education in a few simple lines:

When a child first stands before a teacher,
The teacher does not see the child's inner being.
The child's unseen inner being
Is what holds the child's potential.
The teacher's task is to educate the child
As an individual, in a kind and humane way,
So that each child's potential can be brought forth
And lit up like a shaft of light shining out into the world,
Enabling the child to grow up to be a freethinking adult.

# ACKNOWLEDGEMENTS

Writing an autobiography can be a long and challenging enterprise, and mine has taken some years to come to fruition. I would like to acknowledge many people who, over the years, helped me to realise my educational vision – because it is the fulfilment of my dream that encouraged me to finally produce this book.

To begin at the beginning, I must first thank my remarkable parents who gave me such a loving childhood and family life. And my eight siblings who have always been with me and who have uniquely understood the many challenges I've faced.

Throughout the last forty-six years Sarah has stood beside me and honoured my dedication to creating a school that offers a truly holistic and child-centred education. I could not have trodden a metre of the path I have carved without Sarah by my side. As a wife, mother and a partner in our shared vision of education, I have found the utmost love and inspiration in Sarah. Never wavering and constantly supportive, I thank my devoted wife for what she has tirelessly given and for what she continues to give as a gifted teacher, in teaching children in the way that we both feel is needed in the world. I am filled with praise and gratitude for what she has achieved.

I salute all my children – Maxine, William, Natasha, James and Oliver – who have helped me to become a proud father and a better teacher. They are an example to me and I have learned so much from them. Thank you to my children.

Terry Oldfield has been a stalwart supporter and giver throughout the thirty years of The Acorn School and was very much the person who gave me the courage to found my school. Terry allowed me to educate all five of his children, and as a friend and guide to my principles he has never failed to honour me and my educational vision. His considerable and unfailing support has been instrumental in the school's success, and even after almost four decades of involvement, he is still steadfast and right here with me at the touch of a button. I thank Terry for a deeply enriching friendship and for writing the foreword to the book.

I'm immensely grateful to all those first Acorn parents who took the road less travelled in 1991 and had the courage to enter their children into a new and an unproven educational system. In particular, I thank Janette and Stephen Hall and Alan and Victoria McDonald for their unswerving support and for never failing to stand by me throughout the education of their children. Thank you to Sandra Bruce who enrolled her daughter in 1991 and backed me for the first year, ensuring that Acorn would continue. Also to David and Sue Thomas, whose son came with me from Herefordshire to Acorn. John and Linda Meletiou were totally committed parents, and John was the school administrator for a year, making many improvements and winning the battle against those who tried to prevent me from declaring Acorn to be a Rudolf Steiner inspired school. The strength and support of these parents helped to sustain me in the school's early days.

I also owe a huge debt of gratitude and appreciation to all the parents who have ever chosen, and who are even now in the process of choosing, to send their children to Acorn. Without their commitment and vision, the school could not have survived and could not now continue to thrive.

I want to thank all the students I have ever taught for what they have given and shown me. They made me the teacher I became and gave me the incentive to create the best education I could devise. In particular, my heartfelt thanks to all the Acorn students who have given me great joy and brought my vision to life. It has been an honour and a privilege to have taught them. They all know who they are!

I met Barnaby Franklin as a young boy in my class at Wynstones Steiner School in 1986, and he was an inspiring and enthusiastic student. Barney has been beside me for more than thirty years and is an extraordinary leader and teacher and a good friend. He and I have trodden phenomenal pastures and educated hundreds of children together in all sorts of scenarios, especially on our outward bound adventures. I thank him for supplying the book's section on the school's outdoor activities, weekends away, summer camps and overseas trips. Barney has been a respected and admired Acorn headteacher, and I look forward to his continued presence as our ace gym teacher.

Spanning the past thirty years of Acorn, I would like to thank all of the many Acorn teachers for their outstanding contributions to school life and for wholeheartedly joining me on this adventure. In particular I want to thank the first two pioneering teachers who joined me at Acorn: Lucy de Havas, my first full-time teacher and Sue Meek, my second teacher. Both were loyal and gifted teachers who inspired their pupils and contributed greatly to Acorn with their love and skill.

Working alongside the teaching staff, Acorn has been blessed with exceptional assistance in the school office from two Acorn parents: Pam who handled this demanding role brilliantly for fifteen years, and Grace who is now holding the fort. Grace's unstinting long-term commitment to the school's administration has been a key element in Acorn going forward and evolving with integrity and ease.

Finally I want to acknowledge and thank the people who helped to bring this book together. I found my editor in Katherine, who bravely took on the challenge of turning a pile of disparate notes, written over many years and in different contexts, into some sort of ordered narrative. Countless gaps in the story needed filling – never a problem for me to enthusiastically write more. There was also a frequent need to keep the story on track and direct my exuberant wanderings – more of a challenge! Katherine managed the task admirably, and I thank her for her skill, kindness, patience and tireless sensitivity. Thank you, too, to all those who read earlier versions of the book – Caroline, Annie, Neil, Rosie, Joanna, Natasha, Robyn and Sarah. Their thoughtful feedback proved invaluable. My inestimable gratitude and appreciation goes to my daughter, Natasha, for her enthusiastic encouragement and support and for her key role in organising the photos and production side of the process. Thank you to Jason for his artistry with the cover design. Lastly, my sincere thanks to Bob and Ella and all at YouCaxton for their excellent work and assistance with the self-publication of my book.

# APPENDIX:
# STUDENT TESTIMONIALS

## ANNIE (FORMER ACORN STUDENT)

I attended The Acorn School from age twelve until age nineteen. I thrived in the smaller classes (having been in a class of around 25 previously). Graeme Whiting was an inspiring and charismatic teacher, and I really felt he saw the best in all of us and supported each of us to shine as a person and excel in the subjects we were studying. I was treated with respect for my own individual qualities and interests and felt cared for within the school environment.

During classes, we were encouraged to ask questions, have class discussions and take part in activities which brought each subject alive. I feel I maintained my love of learning and confidence in my ability to be self-motivated and really understand what we learned instead of learning for the sake of a test or exam. I especially enjoyed anatomy and physiology classes with Graeme, and this stood me in good stead for studying for my degree in Herbal Medicine (a BSc Hons) as did the ability to be self-motivated and confident in myself. Despite having never sat an exam before, I managed to get on the course and did well in my degree.

This was all set within a backdrop of the nourishing rhythm of the Acorn ethos, based on the rhythms of nature and the songs, festivals and craft activities associated with each season. I loved learning poems, acting in plays and doing the art, sculpture, mosaic, pottery and stained-glass classes. We even made a wooden Canadian canoe!

I enjoyed physical education classes, especially gymnastics – we used to use a trampette to jump over the tower, do upward circles on the bar, and somersaults on the trampoline as well as from the floor. I also took part in daily circuit-training, which was intense and was a real workout, but felt a good way to start our day. I also loved the Weekends Away canoeing, knee-boarding, hiking with our packs on (with our camping gear) up mountains and on the Isle of Skye. We made camps, cooked our food, sang around the campfire, and played the 'torch game' which involved creeping up on the person with the torch and trying to touch them before they shone the torch on us. Also, I enjoyed our Summer and Winter Camps in Pembrokeshire – sleeping in dorms, swimming in the sea, fishing for mackerel from a canoe, and doing water sports.

I have fond memories of the Italy trips, where we travelled in a minibus through France, Italy and Germany, visiting art galleries as well as many historical sites, including the Colosseum in Rome, the Leaning Tower of Pisa and Vesuvius near Pompeii. There was a sense of camaraderie, humour, fun and the challenges that are all the ingredients of a good adventure!

During my teenage years, the love of learning (and going to school), gymnastics and weekends away were a lifeline to me in an otherwise difficult and stressful time in my life. The physical education and outdoor pursuits provided the challenge and risk-taking element that I felt I needed and that most teenagers need at this time, and if not met in a held way, can mean they are more susceptible to drugs and other destructive pursuits. I feel the physical education gave me a core strength that has served me well in my life, and I continue to value keeping fit and healthy.

The skills I learnt have been so useful and have supported me in my travels, studies, camping trips and now as a parent. I feel I have resources inside myself and skills for which I am continually grateful, and which I can offer my children, the community of people I am connected to and those with whom I work.

## Maxwell (Former Acorn Student)

My time at The Acorn School fits the perfect literary plan for a story. Truly, a beginning, a middle and an end. Due to the bond of friendship and the open mind of Graeme Whiting, this 'story' has not yet ended, despite the fact that I am writing these experiences some time after I left the school. In setting up The Acorn School, Graeme has given an outlet for a unique combination of his life's experiences to become his life's work. From humble beginnings in a poor post-WWII family, he has developed a strength of purpose that has stood him in good stead as an educationist. Graeme has been through untold heartache and a trial of grief and pain; through the shadow of death to a deep-rooted understanding and strength of character, to stand up and manifest what he believes.

This is the backdrop of Graeme's educational mindset, and through consistent hard work and dedication, he has created his own brand of education, a schooling where the student is left free of mind to choose their own life path. This freedom can be a burden, and finding your way can be desperately hard. But with a deep-rooted moral compass that is engaged and engendered in your heart, these gargantuan tasks can be faced; which gives each student a deep-seated confidence and a raft of knowledge to enable them to overcome all the storms and challenges that life will throw at them. I came on the scene in the year 2000.

I arrived at The Acorn School a scared young boy, timid and frail. What struck my mother and me was the harmony that pervaded the school grounds, the happy hubbub of smiling voices and the way that, irrespective of age, from the kindergarten to the tall upper school students, there was respect between each other, from student to student, from teacher to student and most surprisingly, from student to teacher. This was something different. I entered the school and went through this system, which draws on a vast range of educational philosophies, many of which were present in the school at one time or another.

Great store was placed on physical endeavour, both on the field, with a variety of outdoor sports and orienteering, to gymnastics in the school hall; vaulting, trampolining, floor work and trust exercises interwoven with seemingly insurmountable obstacle courses. This trained a great mental and physical resilience which has certainly prepared me for work in HM Government and The British Antarctic Survey.

The Acorn education has Graeme's hallmark all through it; and his integrity. Graeme does away with the usual draconian educational aspirations for the young child. Acorn is the place where people can explore ideas and come to conclusions, rather than being told what to do, what to think and what conclusions to draw! I strongly believe that Graeme and his educational principles will be instrumental and central to the much-needed overhauling of mass education throughout the world. Rather than trying to form children into small adults, Graeme allows children to be what they are: children! The education teaches you where you fit into the world and is a wall of knowledge built from strong foundations.

I have been flabbergasted by the higgledy-piggledy hotchpotch of names and places, which are fundamental in examinations today. Yet these are taught in a disjointed format, for example, today The Battle of the Somme, tomorrow the Battle of Hastings, followed by The Vietnam War. To turn to the 'wall' analogy, how can one expect to build a wall by dropping bricks from ten feet up? If you want a ten-foot wall you have to start with the foundations and then build up. For example, with history, it is taught at Acorn in chronological order enabling the student to think back and gain a thorough understanding as more and more history is learned. You are the spearhead of the events stretched out behind you, and each student is a part of it all. Graeme's educational system allows one to look back in history to the dawn of time. As Churchill said, 'the further you can look back, the further you can see forward.'

Graeme's great understanding of childhood cognitive development has been applied across the educational system at Acorn, and as a result of his research, the labels that are usually pinned on children have been done away with, leading to a great unblocking of many channels. Labels are based on the assumption that all children learn at the same speed and rate, whereas Acorn allows children to develop in their own time, under the guidance of well-trained, sympathetic teachers who understand each child as an individual.

The lessons are based on a threefold system that allows all the range of learning types to connect easily with the subject, and allows the children to engage with all three, instead of being painted into a corner, to be labelled 'thick', 'autistic', 'dyspraxic', 'dyscalculia', 'ADD', 'ADHD' or 'clever'. The school is a place for everyone and there is something for everyone and a place for individuals to shine. It engages kinaesthetic, visual, artistic and intellectual learners, physically engaging the body to learn.

Graeme has the courage of his convictions and is not afraid to speak his mind, nor is he afraid to admit when he is wrong. This is the fluid mind that made him such a successful soldier and makes him such a good role model. I am a young man and we have very few good role models in this world. My alumni of inspiration includes such names as Douglas Bader, Major Dick Winters, Churchill, C.S.Lewis and Tolkien. To this alumni of the world I will forever add the name Graeme Whiting. At the back of Major Winter's book 'Beyond Band of Brothers' can be found a page entitled 'leadership at the point of the bayonet'. With Graeme in mind I offer my summary of this outline of leadership, in a list of points:

Strive to be a leader of competence and courage. Graeme has always exemplified these virtues and encourages them in his students.

Lead from the front, saying, 'follow me'. Graeme has always been at the front, be it in the classroom in front of those he is teaching, or in the lead canoe down the rapids of a river, or in the gymnasium, where I always remember seeing Graeme demonstrate.

Physical stamina is the root of physical toughness. Great store is set by physical endeavour at Acorn, both for boys and girls, and this has encouraged all students to strive for the best they can achieve, and also implants mental competence within them as well as striving for physical excellence and fitness.

Develop your teamwork. The team of teachers is led by Graeme, and he leads this nucleus so that a direction can be established within the school.

Delegate responsibility. Not only does Graeme honour this with his own teachers, but it is imprinted in each student, so they can learn to take on responsibility and rise to unexpected heights in order to take their place in the world.

Anticipate problems. Challenges are to be dealt with and overcome.

Remain humble. Never worry about who receives the credit. Graeme will not be celebrated for what he has brought to the world but will be seen as a visionary in the future. This does not stop Graeme's resolve to pioneer new systems in order to give children back their childhood.

Take time for self-reflection. Graeme is constantly looking at his work and for ways to improve it.

True satisfaction comes from getting the job done! The key to successful leadership is to earn respect. Of all the men I have met, I know Graeme to be the most manly, balanced man and I respect him hugely, and he in turn respects me.

Hang tough! Never, ever give up. Graeme is still pioneering at age seventy-five. He will continue to be unique and will never give up while there is breath in his body.

To quote Churchill again, 'perfection spells paralysis.' There is no perfect educational system, and Graeme will be the first to say that his education is not what everyone will choose, as it demands active interaction and strength – if you are strong and 'hang tough' through his educational system you will be able to truly wear the mantle and responsibility of freedom and know that you are truly alive.

## ROSALIND (FORMER ACORN STUDENT)

We did archery, and sometimes you demonstrated it for us, always hitting the black of course! Most of my memories are of the outdoor activities:

Canadian-canoeing down the River Wye, camping and sleeping rough in forests and on riverbanks, and the singing and life stories around the campfire. On Summer Camp it was knee-boarding on the estuary at Lawrenny, Pembrokeshire; the rock-jumping, with you at the bottom, treading water to make sure we resurfaced safely.

Gosh, the times we had, it seems like a lifetime ago now. You were an inspiration to all of us, setting us challenges and being there to help us overcome them. I am thinking of the mud at Chepstow at low tide for instance, when we had to carry our huge self-made Canadian canoes, sinking into the mud up to our mid-thighs! Back then there were fewer health and safety rules, and we were able to experience real-life situations that were pretty challenging for all of us, which strengthened us, especially as we didn't ever call off a trip, but always saw it through to the end.

I could go on for much longer. There were so many character and group building situations that have had a big impact on me and my life.

### DESMOND (FORMER KINGS LANGLEY STUDENT)

I was a very damaged and sensitive child when I first met Graeme Whiting. Through his disciplined approach and wisdom, but mainly the time he spent with us, we all benefited hugely from his innovative, highly energised and inventive teaching.

Graeme clearly understood the psychology behind everything he was doing which made it an extremely powerful package for a young mind. He got us all involved in a sponsored walk to earn money to buy gym equipment. For me this was one of the first chances I've ever had to prove I could excel at something. I raised quite a lot of money and was extremely motivated to do so. We ended up with a gymnasium full of Olympic-standard equipment which we learned to use to quite a high level. There was also a scaffolding tower which I think was 30 feet high. We would jump from this tower doing forward and backward somersaults onto a trampoline bed covered in crash mats for safety. I can remember the feeling of standing on that tower with my back to the trampoline and the void below and having to find the courage to do a backward somersault from a 30-feet-high tower.

This changed me at a very fundamental level. Not only was I very excited by this, but I was also having to overcome some huge fears, which I did with Graeme's encouragement. And Graeme didn't just talk the talk, he walked it too. I was in desperate need of help, and Graeme and Sarah came to my rescue and helped steer me on a course which I wouldn't otherwise have been able to achieve. Graeme help turn me from a scared, angry little boy into a strong, confident man.

I got on really badly at school, but he was someone who could see through the naughty side of my character and help encourage some real learning. He understood that one needs to look at the whole person, give them some trust and then back them up.

It was an amazing turning point for me and it enabled the good part of my character to thrive.

Graeme has dedicated his life to education, but more than that, he has dedicated his life to the spirit of humanity and to try and kindle the best things in people and for them to then express that in the world.

Thank you, Graeme and Sarah.


## NICHOLAS (FORMER KINGS LANGLEY STUDENT)

Graeme the Circus Ringleader

In the 1970s and early 80s, Graeme was generally to be found in the sports hall of the King's Langley Rudolf Steiner school. A large space, Graeme's location in the room was nonetheless immediately obvious. Whether this was to do with his imposing 'he-man' physique, booming voice, or the constant orbiting buzz of activity is difficult to say. A typical-looking school sports hall at first glance, a more detailed inspection disclosed an array of apparatus that would not have been out of place in a travelling big top. An oversized trampoline with steel springs took centre stage, with a harness suspended above, itself attached to a rope and pulley system fixed to the steel roof struts. Adjacent, 'The Tower', a square metal scaffold complete with wooden boards, two storeys high, from which gymnastically inclined acolytes executed fear defying leaps onto crash mats strategically placed on the trampoline bed below. Scattered around and about were an array of mats, bars, rings, trampettes (including Graeme's precious double trampette which he designed) and various items of vaulting equipment.

An exciting scene for any active boy, I first experienced it at two and a half years of age. This is the earliest and most formative example of cause and effect in my life. The cause being my having a hyperactive disposition, and consequently, a mother at her wits' end. Faced with an unskilled circus performer attempting fear inducing leaps from the sofa to the armchair, my mother quickly realised a trained ringleader was required. Fortuitously, one appeared. Occasional babysitting duties were at that time performed by a young woman called Sarah. Sarah had many qualities. For present purposes the key one is that she was Graeme's girlfriend. The pivotal introduction thus made, I was released into the gym whereupon Graeme found himself in the role of personal trainer to an egocentric, feral force of nature.

Ten years rolled by, during which Graeme's regular ministrations manipulated and moulded this unvarnished bundle of unfocused energy. It takes a skilled master to combine encouragement of a child's natural exuberance whilst simultaneously, noiselessly, teaching discipline. And I am not talking here of physical discipline, but its mental bedfellow. For Graeme has always understood that the mind takes centre stage in all matters, including (and, possibly, especially) where physical activity is called for. As master of gymnastic ceremonies, Graeme taught his disciples to dissolve the disconnect between the brain and the body. Through prior visualisation of the physical in the mind's eye, Graeme taught that the art of execution lies in mental preparation. This lesson pervades life, far beyond the performance of a superficially beguiling gymnastic manoeuvre. It goes to the heart of wellbeing. By aligning the mental and the physical, it facilitates the development of one's whole self. It also leads inexorably to something we might these days call mindfulness.

And what fun too! And so, it would seem, great things can come from jumping off the sofa.


## DAVID (FORMER KINGS LANGLEY STUDENT)

Graeme Whiting mentioned to me once that he wanted to break a world record, so he set about creating the largest long jump pit in the world. And I am not exaggerating – it could have been a swimming pool.

It was a work of love and most days in the Spring of 1976, Graeme was up early in the mornings digging this massive pit. It measured 46' x 22' and was long enough for four jumpers to jump from both directions and never meet. Six children could jump across the pit at one time in complete safety.

The governors and some other teachers of the school didn't support this initiative, and many walked straight past and only glanced at what was being created as more and more earth was dug up and deposited around the huge hole. The younger children just stood watching and staring as each break-time was getting more and more exciting. It took a month for Graeme to create the concrete surrounds alone and finally a lorry brought 9 cubic metres of sand to fill the gigantic pit.

This pit was a much-needed and magical addition to the school grounds and served a great purpose, as the after-school athletics clubs often involved over 100 children. All of this was paid for by a sponsored walk, mostly organised and inspired by one of the pupils. I remember that the school governors didn't pay a penny for this specialised kit, but it was unstoppable as the parents paid the fees and raised the money to pay for it.

Graeme also set up a vast amount of gymnastic equipment in the school gym, aided by many enthusiastic older pupils. We saw him bouncing on the trampoline, performing twisting routines including double-somersaults, and rotating around the equipment as though the Olympics were going to be held in our hall! Once, I entered the gym and although it was silent there were over a hundred children standing and watching as Graeme performed on the parallel bars. He was doing a handstand, and every few seconds he pirouetted a complete 360 degree turn, and then swung down into a reverse somersault dismount.

'What on earth was that?' I asked one senior boy. 'I have no idea' he replied, 'but I want to learn it!' And he did! Graeme christened every piece of equipment with his performance. None of us had ever seen anything like it. Graeme's stunning skills inspired every child in the school, from age six to nineteen, to become gymnasts, and throughout his time at the school there was never a moment of disrespect towards him, including no lateness to lessons. He certainly loved teaching us all, no matter who we were or how capable we were. Graeme always saw the potential in every child he taught. Within a couple of months, the school gym was filled each morning and lunch break with children learning gymnastics. It was always a safe and welcoming place to go to.

Children were heard leaving their classrooms after their first lesson, running helter-skelter to this new centre for physical excellence. The gym clubs were overflowing, and every child was able to join. It was gym for all, always, and the main school seemed to disappear into oblivion in the face of this new impulse that fired our passion.

I will end by thanking Graeme, and Sarah, who he trained, for giving me and all of us a great start in our lives, with confidence and uprightness. He made our school life wonderful, which it certainly was not before he arrived. Graeme changed my life!

I salute you Mr Whiting and respect you with all my heart. I owe you so much for the inspiration you subliminally wove into me and hundreds of other children.


## JEREMY (FORMER DEAN CLOSE STUDENT)

I've worked out that I've known Graeme for 79% of my life. That's a long time. Dates back to when I was 13. So there are lots of memories. But memory is a funny thing, in terms of what stands out when you look back. Here's one early thing that made a big impact on me. It's night time, a car is driving along a back road somewhere in Suffolk or Norfolk, on the way to a lake where we might catch a carp. I'm in the passenger seat, eating fish and chips. And what I should stress is that in those days, when I was a teenager, I was an Olympic standard food scoffer, in terms of both quantity and speed, and I was going at it two-handed, fuelled by several hours of hunger. And when I finished I saw an empty sheet of newspaper beside me. Somehow Graeme had finished his quicker than me, one-handed while driving. It made a big impression on me, and it still does, because it's a small thing that stands for a big thing. Graeme never does things by halves; it's always whole-hearted – whether it's fishing or archery or (why not?) deciding to open your own school.

Fast forward several years and I ended up working at Acorn for 6 months. It started just before the annual art history trip to Italy, and for 2 weeks I taught 20 minutes a day of basic Italian from a book I put together using a very basic language tape. On our first night in Italy, pairs of students were assigned to different houses scattered around Rome, and instructed to make their way to a rendezvous in St Peter's Square the next morning. I remember the last pair we dropped off from the van were doubting their ability to navigate a strange foreign city. And this is where we come to Graeme's way with words, when it comes to cajoling and motivating, and speaking across the generations. 'Just round the corner from here,' he said, 'is the biggest church in the world. Are you telling me you won't be able to find it?' Needless to say, everybody found their way to the rendezvous the next day, and the sense of achievement at meeting this challenge was tangible.

Another small but big thing I remember from this time: I was staying with Graeme's family in their spare room, and one night there were sounds from the garden. Graeme and I went tearing out there in our night clothes and disturbed somebody trying to break into the car. I have to confess that my default reaction to being made to stumble around outside in the dark in my bedroom slippers is to swear a lot. But Graeme is one of the few people I know whose default setting is to laugh at adversity. It comes across, to me, as disbelief at the absurdity of the world. It's something I keep trying to emulate, but most times I fail miserably.

The main thing about Graeme, though, is this. His energy. More specifically, it's a special kind of energy that acts as a catalyst on others. We all have great potential within us, but the difficult thing is activating it. Some people have the gift of providing the necessary spark to others – and this is at the heart of education, as something quite distinct from imparting information, and ultimately more important.

Graeme is one of the rare people with that special gift, and it's something that doesn't get switched off, which is why it's hard to imagine him ever being properly retired.

BV - #0028 - 221122 - C0 - 229/152/14 - PB - 9781914424694 - Matt Lamination